Bringing the

to your Earl

This easy-to-read series provides an introduction to some of the most important early years philosophies and shows how they can be incorporated into your setting. Each book provides:

- an outline of the background to the approach
- clear explanations of the relevance to contemporary thinking
- suggestions to help you plan a successful learning environment
- examples of what the individual approach can look like in practice.

These convenient guides are essential to early years practitioners, students and parents who wish to fully understand what each approach means to their setting and children.

Have you ever wondered about the origins of the kindergarten and the influence of Froebel on early years practice? What did Froebel mean by a 'garden for children'? Why did he believe that play is central in young children's learning?

Bringing the Froebel Approach to your Early Years Practice looks at the founder of the kindergarten and his profound influence on provision and practice for young children today. The Froebelian approach is not a method but includes distinctive principles which shape and guide practice.

This book includes:

- a discussion of key Froebelian principles such as play, imagination, creativity, learning through self-activity and making connections

- an examination of block play and how this can be developed in contemporary settings
- Froebel's ideas on nature and outdoor play and why these are fundamental to young children's learning
- how Froebel used movement, song, rhythm and rhyme to provide key learning experiences
- examples of innovative practice and ideas for further reflection.

This convenient guide will help early years practitioners, students and parents to really understand what the Froebel approach can bring to their practice and children.

Helen Tovey is Principal Lecturer in Early Childhood Studies at the University of Roehampton, London. She is a Froebel-trained nursery teacher, a former headteacher and a Trustee of the National Froebel Foundation. Helen is recognised nationally as an authority on the development of outdoor environments and has published widely.

Bringing the Froebel Approach to your Early Years Practice

Helen Tovey
Series edited by Sandy Green

Routledge
Taylor & Francis Group

LONDON AND NEW YORK

First published 2013
by Routledge
2 Park Square, Milton Park, Abingdon, Oxon OX14 4RN

Simultaneously published in the USA and Canada
by Routledge
711 Third Avenue, New York, NY 10017

Routledge is an imprint of the Taylor & Francis Group, an informa business

British Library Cataloguing in Publication Data
A catalogue record for this book is available from the British Library

Library of Congress Cataloging-in-Publication Data
Tovey, Helen, 1950– author.
Bringing the Froebel approach to your early years practice /
Helen Tovey.
pages cm
Includes bibliographical references.
1. Kindergarten. 2. Child development. 3. Fröbel, Friedrich,
1782–1852. I. Title.
LB1162.T68 2012
372.21'8–dc23
2012016926

ISBN: 978–0–415–56730–5 (hbk)
ISBN: 978–0–415–56731–2 (pbk)
ISBN: 978–0–203–81837–4 (ebk)

Typeset in Optima
by Keystroke, Station Road, Codsall, Wolverhampton

Contents

Acknowledgements

I would like to thank the parents, children and staff from the following early years settings for permission to use photographs and observations:

- Annan Farm – The Froebel Small School, Sussex
- Bayonne Nursery School and Children's Centre, London
- Bridgwater College Children's Centre, Somerset
- the former Redford House Nursery, University of Roehampton
- Somerset Nursery School and Children's Centre, London
- Southway Nursery School, Bedford
- Vanessa Nursery School, London.

Special thanks to Joachim Liebschner – who first inspired my interest in Froebelian ideas as my tutor at the Froebel Educational Institute, London in 1968 – and to Professors Kevin Brehony and Tina Bruce at the University of Roehampton, London, who continue to deepen my understanding of Froebelian principles and practice.

Thanks also to Kornelia Cepok from the Froebel Archive for Childhood Studies at the University of Roehampton, London for permission to use Figures 2.1 and 2.2 from the Archive collection, to Lucy Parker for Figure 5.7, Debbie Hunter for Figure 8.4 and to Dr Jane Read, Senior Lecturer at the University of Roehampton, for feedback on draft chapters.

An introduction to a Froebelian approach

Friedrich Froebel (1782–1852), a nineteenth-century German educator, was arguably the most significant of the pioneers of early childhood education and care. He created the first kindergarten, a garden or nursery where young children could grow and develop at their own pace, nurtured by knowledgeable and supportive adults. This was at a time when there was almost no provision for young children. Froebel argued that the earliest years of a child's life are the most important in a child's education and lay the foundation for all later learning. Young children, he argued, learn best through self-activity, talk and play. These ideas, although widely accepted today, were radical concepts in Froebel's time.

Although the word 'kindergarten' is widely known today, the name 'Froebel' is less well known. Yet many of the resources which we take for granted today – such as blocks, sand, water, clay, finger rhymes, painting and drawing and outdoor play – and practices such as observation-led planning and partnerships with parents and community are closely linked to Froebel's ideas. He was unique in the way he integrated these resources and practices into a coherent pedagogical approach.

However, although many of Froebel's ideas have become mainstream today, the values which underpin them are not always well understood, leading to widely differing interpretations and practices. This makes it all the more important to look at the broad principles which underpin Froebelian ideas and to consider them in relation to current practice.

An approach, not a method

A Froebelian approach is not a method. There is no formula or recipe to follow or set of equipment to purchase or prescribed curriculum to adhere to. Nor is it a series of ideas and activities which practitioners can dip in and out of. Rather it is a whole way of thinking about children and childhood, based on a set of values and principles. A Froebelian approach may resonate and overlap with other progressive approaches, but it also has some features which are distinctive.

A Froebelian approach

A Froebelian approach is underpinned by the key principles explained below. A more extensive list of Froebelian principles can be found in Appendix 1 (pp. 124–126).

Respect

A Froebelian approach is inherently respectful of young children. It views children as powerful learners, motivated from birth to explore, investigate and be curious about the world and to try, through their own efforts, to understand it. Education should build on this powerful urge to learn.

Connectedness

Learning should be meaningful and connected to children's own experiences. It should not be divided up into subjects but should be experienced as a meaningful whole so that children can connect new ideas to what they already know. A view of the whole child is paramount, for everything is linked.

Play, talk and first-hand experiences

Play, talk and first-hand experiences are central to young children's learning. Play integrates all learning and is the leading form of development in children, allowing them to operate at their highest level.

Creativity

Creativity is the essence of being human and is fundamental to learning. Creativity enables children to make connections between their inner world of feelings and ideas and their outer world of things and experiences, and to reflect on them both. Play, imagination and symbolic representation are important features of creativity.

Freedom and guidance

Free movement, free choice and self-activity are important, but they should be within a framework of guidance in which the role of the adult is crucial.

Play outdoors

Direct, everyday experience of the natural world outdoors is essential so that children can learn to appreciate its wonders and begin to understand the interrelationship between all living things. The nursery garden is a rich environment offering potential for all areas of learning.

Community

Nurseries and schools should be democratic, respectful communities of learners, where adults and children can learn from each other. They should be closely connected to the wider community of people and places.

Positive relationships

Relationships with children should be close, trusting, responsive, interactive and intellectually engaging. They should build on the positive characteristics of each individual child, extending what they can already do, rather than what they are not yet able to do.

Well-informed and qualified educators

The care and education of young children is essential to society. Young children are entitled to knowledgeable and well-qualified professionals who are deeply informed about and attuned to the distinctive nature of young children's learning and development. Practitioners must constantly strive to develop their understanding through training, observation, research, reflection and discussion.

Froebelian principles today

Many of Froebel's ideas are now part of mainstream thinking. For example, his core principles underpin much of the revised Early Years Foundation Stage in England, with its four guiding themes of the Unique Child, Positive Relationships, Enabling Environments indoors and outdoors and the interconnectedness of all areas of Learning and Development (DfE 2012). Play, creativity, partnerships, community, observation-led planning, and well-informed and reflective educators are also key features of the Early Years Foundation Stage guidance.

However, there are also aspects of policy and practice today which do not reflect Froebel's principles. For example, the current emphasis on 'school readiness' runs counter to Froebel's belief that the best preparation for the next phase of learning is to have the richest and most appropriate experiences in the earlier phases, rather than just 'preparing' children for something to come.

It is also possible to find examples of practice which are far from Froebel's principles, where learning is driven by outcomes and targets rather than children's powerful urge to learn. Children can be hurried on to the next stage of learning, given activities which have little meaning to them, spend long periods of time sitting listening to adults or given dull, passive occupational activities. In some settings children spend much of their day indoors in plasticised environments, cut off from the natural world or from authentic first-hand experience.

Such practices are not compatible with a Froebelian approach, and serve as a reminder that at any time in history there is a need for advocates who can champion the rights of young children and seek to enrich their lives and learning.

Part of an evolving tradition of early childhood education

A Froebelian approach is not about looking back and trying to preserve outdated theories and practices from the past. Rather it is about deepening our understanding of the roots of current ideas and practices in ways which can help us move forward with more strength and confidence. It is part of a tradition of progressive ideas which has evolved over time. It is not a static, rigid approach.

Froebel himself drew on the ideas of Rousseau and Pestalozzi, as well as the prominent philosophers and writers of his day. Other pioneering educators – including Margaret McMillan, Susan Isaacs, Rudolph Steiner and Loris Malaguzzi – built on Froebel's ideas but also developed their own distinctive features of philosophy and practice.

Froebel argued that that we should acknowledge past ideas, as it is from them that all new growth emerges:

> We cannot tear the present from the past or from the future. Past, present and future are the trinity of time. The future demands the renewing of life, which must begin in the present. In the children lies the seed-corn of the future.
> (Froebel, cited in Marenholtz-Bülow 1891: 4)

As you think about the ideas in this book and use them to reflect on, question and develop your practice, you can contribute to this rich tradition of ideas and help shape the ideas and practice of the future.

Using the Froebel approach to reflect on your practice

- What are the key principles which shape your approach to children and families? How are they similar to or different from Froebelian principles?

- What connections can you see between Froebelian principles and the Early Years Foundation Stage (DfE 2012)?

- Where do your ideas come from? Who has been the biggest influence on your philosophy and practice?

2 | Friedrich Froebel, his life and his ideas

I wanted to educate men to be free, to think, to take action for themselves.

(Froebel, in Lilley 1967: 41)

Froebel's early life

Friedrich Froebel was born in 1782 in Oberweissbach, a small town in the Thuringian Forest in what is now Germany. His mother died when he was 8 months old and he spent a lonely, isolated early childhood, looked after by servants and his five older brothers. His father, a strict Lutheran pastor, was so occupied with his religious duties that he had little time to spend with the young Friedrich. It appears the young boy was often in trouble and could do little to please his father and step-mother. In his autobiography he refers to the 'gloomy, lowering dawn' of his early life (Froebel 1886: 9). His isolation was made worse by his stepmother's indifference and eventual rejection of him. He became an introspective child, spending much time on his own in the parsonage garden, in close contact with the natural world of plants, birds and insects. Here he developed the lifelong love of nature which was to shape his educational ideas.

Friedrich's life changed when, at 10 years old, he went to live with a maternal uncle. His uncle was also a pastor but more gentle and kind than Friedrich's own father and someone who put a loving religion into

Figure 2.1 Friedrich Froebel as a young man.

practice, showing the young boy the patience and affection which had been lacking from his earlier life. Here he experienced much greater freedom, attending school, playing with boys of his own age and roaming the surrounding countryside. Froebel later claimed that the contrast between the two family environments had a profound effect on the growth of his educational ideas (Froebel 1886).

Froebel left school at 15 with an aptitude for mathematics and an intense love of the natural world. He spent two years apprenticed to a forester where he was largely left to himself but where he began the long process of self-education by studying texts on botany, classifying plants and trees and engaging in long walks through the woods. Even at this young age, Froebel was searching for the meaning of life, the nature of mankind, and the spiritual unity which he believed connected all existence. An opportunity to study at Jena University, then a centre of new, radical philosophical ideas, opened up a range of areas of study but this was to end after two years when Froebel was sent to the university prison for unpaid debts. These were caused partly by his generosity in lending money to others and partly by his apparent lack of concern over practical matters such as finance, which continued throughout his life.

Froebel studied an eclectic mix of subjects including botany, mathematics, architecture and crystallography. Most of these were self-taught. Studying crystals was highly significant to Froebel as he believed that crystals revealed the universal patterns of life in their growth of form, beauty and harmony. After working as a curator in a mineral museum, he had many different occupations including tutoring, farming and also as a soldier in the Prussian army fighting Napoleon. On the verge of taking up a career in architecture, he decided to pursue his ideals in education after working at the progressive Frankfurt School run by a former pupil of Pestalozzi. Froebel was impressed by Pestalozzi's ideas on active learning and direct experience and Pestalozzi was a formative influence on his ideas. However, Froebel eventually rejected Pestalozzi's approach as lacking an overall coherence and for keeping separate, rather than integrating, subject areas.

Froebel formed his own school for children from 7 years old, at Keilhau in Thuringia. This was a democratic community where adults and children lived together in harmony, sharing the community tasks of working on the farm, tending the animals and growing fruit and vegetables for the school kitchens. There was a respectful approach to discipline and, where necessary, children and staff would discuss and decide an appropriate consequence for any misbehaviour. Children and teachers spent much time outdoors learning geography, history, science and nature in practical ways, mapping the local area from the hilltops, damming up streams, and acting out battle scenes from history. Festivals were celebrated, and music, songs, dance and drama were central to the community life. Education was active, meaningful and engaging (Liebschner 1992).

However, Froebel increasingly realised that education would never be a force for regenerating society unless there was provision for the youngest children. The early years of life, he concluded, are the most powerful and influential and they are the foundation on which all later learning is built.

The birth of the kindergarten

It was not until he was in his mid-fifties that Froebel found his real passion, the education of the very youngest children. The first 'kinder-garten' opened in 1837 in Bad Blankenburg, a small village close to the Thuringian mountains in what was then Prussia. Froebel recalls in his autobiography how he struggled for a few years to find an appro-priate name for his new venture as he did not want to use the word 'institution' or 'school' which implied more formal schooling and institutional life. Rather he saw it as a community where children could grow and learn at their own pace, with adults who understood their development and cultivated their learning, just as good gardeners tend young plants. He gained inspiration as he was walking with a colleague in the beautiful Thuringian mountains and he shouted out to the hills,

Eureka! I have it! Kindergarten shall be the name.

Froebel (1886: 137)

The word 'kindergarten' combined the human (*kinder*) with the natural (*garten*) and it could mean both a 'garden *of* children' and a 'garden *for* children' (Weston 2000). The word captured Froebel's vision of a place which was in tune with the natural development of children, where they could grow and develop in harmony with nature, a place which cultivated the unique capacities of each individual as part of a community of learners.

About fifty young children between the ages of 2 and 7 attended the kindergarten. It was situated in the village square in Blankenburg, so was a central part of the community and easily accessible to children and families. The kindergarten was inclusive, unlike the schools of the time which were segregated by class or religion. It was open from 6 a.m. until 7 p.m., offering flexible provision for working parents. Children brought sandwiches which were shared together, and clean, mended clothes were available for the poorest children. Many children had to be washed in the village fountain before going in (Weston 2000).

The 'gifts and occupations'

The kindergarten was resourced with specially devised materials for children's play and learning which Froebel called 'gifts and occupations'. These included small soft crocheted balls on string, wooden blocks, materials for weaving, sewing, drawing and painting, wooden pattern boards, peas and sticks for constructing, and clay, sand and water. (See Chapter 5 for details about the gifts and occupations.) Stories, circle games, singing, dancing, music and finger rhymes were important parts of the day.

Froebel set up a community workshop for the production of his educational materials and installed a press to print explanations on their use. The most skilled carpenters and printers were employed, as the aesthetics of the materials were very significant to Froebel. It was also important that everyone understood the purpose and value of the materials they were making. This was a real community endeavour.

The garden

The kindergarten included a garden area for play outdoors and enough space so that each child had their own plot of land for gardening. Here they could sow seeds, tend the plants and harvest the produce, developing an awareness of the cycles of life and the changing seasons. The small individual gardens, each with its wooden name label, were encircled by the communal gardens. Children were free to plant what they liked in their own gardens but were expected to share in the care of the communal gardens. This illustrated Froebel's educational philosophy which emphasised the individual at the heart of a loving whole community, and freedom tempered by responsibility.

Froebel, based on his detailed observations of babies, understood that learning starts at birth and that parents, particularly mothers, are their children's first educators and must be involved in children's learning. He devised a series of songs and rhymes, the forerunners of

Figure 2.2 The garden in Froebel's kindergarten at Blankenberg.

today's finger rhymes and action songs, for mothers to share with their babies and toddlers at home. Mothers and educators working together could be a powerful force of change in society he argued. It was in the publication of the 'Mother Songs' that Froebel brought together all his educational ideas, and he claimed it as his finest achievement.

Education, training and the importance of women educators

Froebel promoted his educational ideas on the kindergarten through lecture tours, articles, open letters and weekly newspapers. His ideas spread rapidly and within ten years there were more than fifty kindergartens in Germany. He realised that transforming the education of young children required teachers who were deeply knowledgeable about young children's development and learning.

At that time teaching was an all-male profession and it was considered unacceptable for women to work professionally outside the home. However, Froebel believed that education would never succeed unless it included women. He put forward his ideas at an education conference but they were ridiculed, and his speech was 'drowned by the laughter of the all-male audience' (Liebschner 1992: 28). Despite this, Froebel succeeded in setting up the first specialist training college for women kindergarten teachers in Europe, offering certified courses in the Froebel approach. Clearly Froebel was way ahead of his time in promoting the role of women as educators but his rather idolised view of women as the best teachers of young children may also have contributed to the gender imbalance in the early years workforce which is so evident today.

One of his ardent followers, Baroness von Marenholtz-Bülow, dedicated her life to spreading the kindergarten movement, undertaking lecture tours throughout Europe and setting up training colleges. She describes her first meeting with Froebel, who was known by some as 'the old fool':

> I met on my walk this so called 'old fool'. A tall, spare man, with long gray hair, was leading a troop of village children between the ages

of three and eight, most of them barefooted and but scantily clothed, who marched two and two up a hill, where, having marshalled them for a play, he practised with them a song belonging to it. The loving patience and abandon with which he did this, the whole bearing of the man while the children played various games under his direction, were so moving, that tears came into my companion's eyes as well as into my own and I said to her 'This man is called "an old fool" by these people; perhaps he is one of those men who are ridiculed . . . by contemporaries, and to whom future generations build monuments'.

(Marenholtz-Bülow 1891: 1–2)

Closure of the kindergartens

Through his work Froebel convinced many others of the significance of his educational ideas. But he also experienced ridicule, criticism and hostility, particularly from the orthodox church which accused him of heresy.

The Prussian court was suspicious of Froebel's aim of developing free, thinking, independent people. In 1851 it imposed a 'Kindergarten Verboten' banning order, believing – mistakenly – that the kindergartens were a front for atheist and socialist ideas. All kindergartens were closed and Froebel did not live to see the ban lifted. He died in 1852.

Spread of Froebel's ideas

Not surprisingly, attempts to suppress Froebel's educational approach had the opposite effect. Many of his followers and trained kindergarten teachers left Germany and set up kindergartens and training courses across Europe, America and Asia.

In England the Froebel Society (founded in 1874) and the National Froebel Union (founded in 1887) were especially influential in training teachers and promoting Froebel's ideas. They later combined to form the National Froebel Foundation which is still active today in promoting Froebelian ideas and supporting research, scholarship, training, conferences and educational projects, including an innovative project in Soweto, South Africa (see Louis 2012).

The Froebel Educational Institute, now part of Roehampton University, London, was founded in 1892 and the three-year training course was highly regarded as the specialist course for teachers of young children. Today, there are Froebel Certificate Courses at Roehampton, London, Edinburgh and Canterbury Christchurch universities. They examine Froebelian ideas in a contemporary context and help practitioners to reflect on and develop their own practice.

Froebel's ideas helped shape the ideas of other nursery pioneers – for example, Margaret McMillan, who developed the English Nursery Schools, was a member of the Froebel Society for many years. Susan Isaacs, researcher, teacher and first director of the Child Development Unit at the University of London, also drew strongly on Froebelian ideas.

Froebelians had a strong influence on the development of policy and practice for young children. Their ideas can be found in many UK government reports, including the Hadow Report (1933), the Plowden Report (1967), the Curriculum Guidance for the Foundation Stage (2000), Birth to Three Matters (2002) and Early Years Foundation Stage (2007).

Today there are very few schools called 'Froebel' schools, compared with say 'Steiner' or 'Montessori' schools. Froebel wanted his ideas to be accepted by all rather than seen as a separate 'method'. Froebelian practice remains closely linked with high-quality provision today and many Froebel-trained educators are influential in the leadership of nursery schools and children's centres, university Early Childhood Studies degree programmes and in many key local authority advisory and inspection roles.

Froebel's ideas are embedded in many approaches and practices today. They have been enriched over time by other significant pioneers of early childhood and through deepening understanding of young children and their lives, learning, emotions and relationships. However, some ideas have become diluted or muddled over time and detached from the principles which once underpinned them. The chapters that follow look more closely at Froebel's ideas in a contemporary context.

A Froebelian approach to play and learning

3

> Play is the highest level of child development. It is the spontaneous expression of thought and feeling – an expression which his inner life requires . . . It promotes enjoyment, satisfaction, serenity, and constitutes the source of all that can benefit the child . . . At this age play is never trivial; it is serious and deeply significant.
>
> (Froebel, in Lilley 1967: 84)

Froebel developed his ideas on play from observing children closely and by thinking about and reflecting on play in relation to the ideas of his time. So what did Froebel believe was the deep significance of play?

Froebel's ideas on play

- Play builds on the young child's innate impetus for self-activity.

- In play the whole child is active – moving, feeling, thinking and willing are integrated.

- Self-chosen play activities help develop determination, concentration and persistence.

- Play helps children reflect on and understand themselves as well as the world around them. It makes the 'outer' inner and the 'inner' outer.

- Play is increasingly social and fosters friendship, fairness, understanding of rules and care for others.

- Play encourages close relationships between adults and children. It helps adults gain insight into the minds and future minds of children.

- Play helps develop an awareness of symbols and symbolic thought where children operate at their highest level.

- Adults have a critical role in valuing, supporting and extending play through the provision of play material, indoors and outdoors, and through informed, sensitive observation and interaction.

- When children have little or no opportunity for play, the pattern of their development can be disturbed and distorted.

(Adapted from Froebel's writings, in Lilley 1967)

Froebel's ideas on play anticipated those of Vygotsky, who also argued that 'play is the leading form of development in young children' (1978: 70). Similarly, the Early Years Foundation Stage states that 'in their play children play at their highest level' (DCSF 2008: 4.1).

Free-flow play

Tina Bruce, a prominent Froebelian educator and author, identifies what she calls 'free-flow play'. This view of play emphasises the freedom which is essential in play, for children to choose, take control, explore, create, imagine and go beyond the here and now. It also emphasises the importance of 'flow' – the intense focused involvement experienced when the players are totally absorbed in the play and which can bring great satisfaction. The term 'free-flow' also refers to the dynamic quality of play. Play flows, often in unpredictable ways, through space and over time, indoors and outdoors. It connects different aspects of experience and ideas.

Bruce draws on Froebel's ideas as well as on current theory and research to identify twelve key features of free-flow play. She emphasises the choice and control in play, the absence of any pressure to conform to external rules and the importance of children keeping hold of their own play agenda so that it is not taken over by adults. Rich play develops when adults and children play together, respecting each other's ideas./ Play takes children into a world of pretence where they imagine other worlds and create stories of possible and imagined worlds beyond the here and now./

Bruce argues that play is an integrating mechanism which helps children coordinate their ideas and feelings and make sense of their relationships with family, friends and culture. Play promotes flexible, adaptive, imaginative, innovative behaviour and makes children into whole people, able to keep balancing their lives in a fast-changing world (Bruce 2004: 149–150, 2011a: 58–59).

Play builds on rich first-hand experience

Although play is central to a Froebelian approach, the provision of play materials alone is not sufficient. Play thrives on first-hand experience and it is this which children draw on in their play. Froebel noted that 'play, which reflects the free activity of the child's mind, must give back again that which education and experience have taught him' (Froebel,

Figure 3.1 Play thrives on rich first-hand experience.

in Lilley 1967: 167). This means that play is a way of drawing together aspects of experience and learning and reflecting on them.

In a Froebelian approach, meaningful, authentic new experiences are carefully planned to extend children's understanding and provide a rich resource for play. This can be seen in the following example.

A nursery school in London used an incubator to hatch chicken's eggs. The children were involved in marking the eggs with a circle or a cross, turning the eggs twice daily, spraying them with water, watching the embryo develop. They listened to the tapping of the beak on the shell and watched the eventual cracking and hatching of the chicks. The children helped care for the newly hatched chicks and observed their development before returning the chicks to a local farm. This was a very powerful experience which provoked much talk, play and representation.

Otis, aged 4, drew the chicks hatching out of the eggs, showing the passage of time from initial cracking to eventual hatching (Figure 3.2). On seeing the drawing, his mother told us that she had seen him playing with a friend in a cupboard at home. They hid quietly in the dark cupboard before dramatically throwing open the cupboard doors and jumping out. Asked what they were doing in the cupboard, Otis replied, 'We were being chicks and waiting twenty-one days to hatch'.

This example illustrates the connection between a powerful first-hand experience, spontaneous play and representation. Play and drawing are tools for thinking about and trying to understand an aspect of experience – waiting a long time, the chick enclosed in the darkness of the egg, inside the incubator then bursting out into space and light. Through play, talk and representation Otis selected an aspect of experience and made it his own, reflecting on it, clarifying it to himself and communicating it to others. This is what Froebel meant when he referred to making the outer world inner, and the inner world outer – and being able to see a connection between the two. /

Within this example there are some important principles of a Froebelian approach to play:

- Rich first-hand experience is a significant resource for play.

Figure 3.2 Representing the chicks hatching out of eggs
in the incubator and the passage of time.

- Play helps build connections between the outer world of new experiences and the inner world of ideas and feelings.

- Representation using different media, in this case talk, drawing and dramatic play, deepens understanding.

Exploring, experimenting and trying things out

Play allows children to be active, to take control, to explore, experiment and try things out. Play allows children to set and pursue their own tasks and to solve problems which are real and meaningful to them. In the course of their play children develop their understanding of the world and of themselves.

Example 1

The children in Figure 3.3 tried to collect water from a small water fountain, using a bucket. However, every time they tipped the bucket the water ran out and they were left with nothing. This was a problem. They found a plastic tube nearby and with much difficulty they attached a tube to the water fountain and then worked together to get the water to flow through the tube into the bucket. They noticed that when the tube was lifted, the water stopped flowing and when the tube was lowered the flow of water returned.

Figure 3.3 Finding and solving problems together.

In this example the children collaborate together to solve a problem which is meaningful to them. They learn through trial and error and repetition. They have an emerging understanding of a relationship between the height of the tube and the flow of the water but it will take much more experience before this cause and effect relationship is well understood.

Within this example there are some important principles of a Froebelian approach to play:

- Time for play helps develop persistence, concentration and determination.

- Play encourages collaborative problem solving and sharing of ideas.

- Play helps adults understand children's emerging ideas of how and why things work.

Example 2

The 2-year-old boy in Figure 3.4 was fascinated by the spiral movement of the water in the fountain. He picked a daisy and dropped it on the water, watching the spiralling movement as the daisy spun round in the water. His attention was focused and intent. He repeated his experiment over and over again, fetching more daisies to drop on the water and sharing his excitement with his friend.

In this example a 2-year-old is deeply involved in a self-chosen task and is not distracted by things happening around him. Play allows him to

Figure 3.4 Play allows this 2-year-old to wonder 'what if?'

wonder 'what if?' – to try things out and repeat his experiment over and over again. Further observation may reveal a pattern to his play, with persistent interest in things that rotate. Research from the Froebel Early Education project directed by Chris Athey (2007) identified a fascination with things that rotate as one of the schemas or patterns of repeatable behaviour that is evident in young children's play. A Froebelian approach is to observe, identify particular schemas and extend them in worthwhile ways, for example by making further provision of things that spin round.

Within this example there are some important principles of a Froebelian approach to play:

- Informed observation is valuable in identifying possible patterns in children's play.

- Play allows children to wonder 'what if?' and repeat their experiments over and over again.

- Adults can tune into children's fascinations and 'persistent concerns' (Athey 2007).

- Adults can extend children's play in worthwhile ways.

Playing imaginatively and developing symbolic thought

Three-year-old Lorenzo loved to play 'going to bed' with an old cardboard box outdoors on the grass. The play involved crawling into the box, shutting the flaps (blinds) and saying 'night night' to the adult playing with him. After a long pause the flaps were thrown open with loud exclamations of 'it's morning time'. They both ate breakfast using a leaf for toast, a small twig for a knife, and poured imaginary milk into imaginary cups. Later, the box became the TV and a small mark on the side of the box was used as the on/off switch. They stared at the rectangular shape as Lorenzo joyfully described the programmes and characters. After an imaginary bath, with lots of rubbing with pretend shampoo and using petals for pretend soap, the twigs came into use again as toothbrushes, on to which was squeezed imaginary toothpaste before the 'going to bed' ritual was enacted again. This play was varied and repeated again and again.

In this example Lorenzo is a confident user of symbols – using objects to stand for something else. A familiar and everyday event in his life can be replayed and varied, as long as the logic of the sequence is followed. 'No, it's not bed time we haven't had our bath yet.' Lorenzo is learning that he can shape the play and can accept or reject the ideas of the adult.

Significantly, he is experiencing the joy of entering into the conspiracy of pretence with another player, when minds meet in an imagined world at the same time as objects are manipulated in the real world. He is learning to think in flexible, abstract ways rather than being constrained by everyday reality.

Within this example there are some important principles of a Froebelian approach to play:

- the immense significance of play in helping develop symbolic thought and abstract thinking

- the value of adults and children playing together, as long as the child keeps control of the play agenda

- the importance of open-ended, freely available materials as rich and flexible resources for play.

Play and storytelling

What is this play of the little ones? It is the great drama of life itself.
(Froebel, cited in Liebschner 1992: 21)

Narrative and storytelling underpin much of children's pretend play, particularly when children play with 'small world' props or collaborate together in a shared play scenario. They spend much time negotiating the characters, plots and scripts of the play, as well as acting within it.

A group of boys used the hollow trunk of a dead willow tree as a prop for their play (Figure 3.5). They filled the space with blue ceanothus flowers from a nearby bush. First they made poison, then magic medicine. A complex narrative unfolds:

Boy A: Let's say this is the cave and the big bad wolf lives here.
Boy B: Yeah and he has poison.
Boy A: Yeah and he has poison plants which kill people.
Boy B: Yeah and he poisons people, poisons people, poisons people.
Boy A: Yeah and they die like this (gestures with his hand to his throat). Don't they?
Boy C: But the magic medicine makes them OK again, doesn't it?
Boy A: No, we haven't got magic medicine.
Boy C: Mix it. We need to mix it.
Boy A: Yeah we need water, don't we? (He fetches a small cup, transforms a piece of bark into a tap and fills the cup with pretend water which is then poured into the tree trunk.)
Boy B: Magic medicine, magic medicine, magic . . .
Boy C: I'll put a spell on you!
Boy A: I'll put a spell on you!
Boy A: The wicked wolf can catch you and eat you up.
Boy B: Yeah, eat you up.
Boy C: But magic medicine makes you 'live again.

In this extract from a long episode of exciting play, the boys are involved in using symbols – transforming simple features of their environment into props for their play. They are negotiating, at an abstract level, the scene, characters and plot for their story. They enjoy the alliterative power of language in their repetition of 'poison plants' and 'magic medicine'. They are exploring universal themes of good and evil, life and death, capture and rescue. All these are significant features which underpin 'storying' and emerging literacy.

The boys' story is acknowledged, valued and written down to be discussed at a later time. This helps to reinforce the idea that the boys are good storymakers and therefore can become good storywriters. This

Figure 3.5 A hollow tree trunk offers many opportunities
for play and storytelling.

Figure 3.6 [Inset] Using symbols – transforming a piece
of bark into a pretend tap.

is very different from approaches that ignore or reject many of the themes of boys' play or which restrict such play with requests to 'stop that, play nicely'.

Play reflects on the big themes of life and death, good and evil, courage and fear, power and weakness.

> If we fail to nurture this deep abiding need of children to play in this way we do them harm . . . it is a powerful way for children to learn very deeply about the nature of friendship, to understand emotions, to represent, to create, to think, to empathize, to develop as talkers, writers and readers.
>
> (Tess Robson, cited in Trudell 2010: 209)

Within this example there are some important principles of a Froebelian approach to play:

- In their free play, children can explore powerful themes and emotions. Recognising and working with such themes is important so that some boys' play in particular is not marginalised.

- Close observation helps adults tune in to and understand the themes of the play.

- Children use features of their environment as symbols in their play.

- Play includes plots, characters and scripts and is strongly linked with narrative and emerging literacy.

Playing with ideas

Children play with ideas as well as with things around them. As soon as they know how something is meant to be it is fun to turn it around and to play with it. They turn ideas upside down, make nonsense and enjoy the ridiculous and the absurd, at the same time recognising the sense behind the nonsense. This love of nonsense is a characteristic of childhood, whether 2-year-olds laughing as they put socks on their hands and gloves on their feet or 4-year-olds enjoying making up new words, as in this cheeky play with words:

Ickety, pickety pop, the dog has swallowed the mop,
Ickety pickety poo, the dog has swallowed you,
Ickety pickety wee, the dog has swallowed me.

Such playful exchanges often focus on rules, make connections between different aspects of experience and create enjoyable absurdities. The following example illustrates how play with ideas builds connections.

Laura, aged 5, wrote a story about a playgroup which was on fire (Figure 3.7). The people dialled 666 to call the police – and the policeman arrived upside down. Here, Laura knows that 666 is 999 upside down. She uses this knowledge to create an incongruous image which has the semblance of a logical connection but clearly is not. She can mentally reverse numbers and ideas and play with them. The resulting idea is fun to share with others.

Figure 3.7 Playing with ideas, turning things
upside down and making nonsense.

Such play with ideas develops into philosophical wonderings as children increasingly explore the world through language. A 4-year-old girl played with what she knew about hot and cold as she washed her hands at the sink.

Hot and cold make warm doesn't it? But when you have warm you can't get the hot and cold back again, can you?

Within these examples there are some important principles of a Froebelian approach to play:

- Children are encouraged to push out boundaries and toy with ideas.

- Play helps develop flexible, innovative, creative ways of thinking.

- Play helps children to know things in deeper and more reflective ways.

- An atmosphere of playful nonsense can be an important way of building close relationships.

Making effective provision for play

A Froebelian approach places a strong emphasis on rich first-hand experience, a challenging play environment, and informed, sensitive adult interaction.

Making time

A Froebelian setting is organised to ensure extended periods of time for play. Play needs time to get going and develop. It does not thrive if it is squeezed into short time slots. Even when time is available, constant interruptions can disrupt play and inhibit its potential. In contrast, extended periods of uninterrupted time allow for engagement and involvement.

Making space

Play needs sufficient space both indoors and outdoors. Such space should be flexible and adaptable to reflect the unpredictable and idiosyncratic nature of play which ebbs and flows in many possible directions. Play also requires a mental space where it is permissible to be creative and toy with ideas, where laughter and humour are valued, not frowned upon as 'being silly'.

Allowing play to flow through space and over time

Froebel argued that all play links and connects. Play is not static and what might start in one area can quickly flow into other areas:

Two 3-year-old boys mixed water and sand together to make 'dinner'. They spread the mixture in some flat boxes and then fetched bottle tops and small pieces of coloured paper from the nearby workshop area to sprinkle on the top. These were taken to the block area, slid inside a hollow block to 'cook' and then transported around the garden on trucks before being delivered to the home corner with a flourishing announcement of 'Pizza delivery!'

Here, the adult supported the logical sequence of the play and allowed it to develop complexity. Where adults insist that materials always stay in their allotted area and are used only for one purpose then play can lack complexity and become stuck and stereotyped. Adults can help children understand that some resources can be moved and returned to their place of storage whereas other more precious resources need to stay put.

Giving play status

Children quickly learn how adults view play. If adults rarely engage with play, are mentally absent when watching play or require work to be completed before play can begin, then this sends strong signals that play has little value and that real learning happens elsewhere. Similarly when adults over-organise and direct the play or insist on achieving pre-planned learning outcomes, then children begin to see that their own ideas are of little value and that play is something that adults organise and control.

Documenting play through photos, books, displays, video and PowerPoint presentations allows it to be shared and discussed with parents, visitors and the local community. Some Froebelians have set up exhibitions on aspects of play in local libraries or community centres. Froebel took children to play in the village square so that he could explain the value of play to local people.

Ensuring a rich play culture

Play thrives in a culture where imagination and creativity are valued, where there is a shared sense of joy in wondering and discovering, where relationships are warm and responsive and where both adults and children are willing to take some risks and be adventurous.

A literacy-rich environment of exciting stories, scripts, characters and plots provides a shared context for children to use and adapt for their own play scenarios. Stories enrich play but play also enriches storytelling as children accumulate a bank of draft scripts, plots and characters which they can use in their storymaking.

Observing, supporting and extending the play

Bruce argues that the role of the adult is to 'observe, support and extend' (Bruce 1997: 97). This appears deceptively simple yet is extra-ordinarily complex. It requires knowledge of children's play, openness to its themes, a willingness to relinquish control, and the sensitivity to see when players are best left alone or when they may need some support. Informed observation is central and helps adults to understand children's learning and make connections with areas of the curriculum where appropriate. Children require both the freedom to pursue their own ideas as well as the support and guidance of adults. Chapter 10 examines the role of the adult in more depth.

Conclusion

This chapter has examined the significant contribution that Froebel and Froebelians today have made to our thinking about play. A Froebel approach is not about directed, guided, overly structured or planned play. It is not about adult tasks dressed up as 'playful learning'. Nor is it about leaving children to play on their own while adults do something else. Rather, it is about starting where children are in their play, but recognising the power of play to take children to new levels of thinking, feeling, imagining, creating and communicating. It is about developing play in ways that are meaningful and supportive and which allow children to keep control of their own play. Play requires a rich environment to flourish and this is the focus of the next chapter.

Bringing a Froebel approach to play and learning

• Do children in your setting get really engrossed in self-chosen activity? Can play 'flow' or is it frequently interrupted?

• How can you foster toddlers' and young children's symbolic play? Are there sufficient open-ended resources for children to transform? Do adults model pretend play?

• Can children play with ideas as well as things? How do adults respond to children's playful nonsense? Is it considered 'silly' or an important tool for learning?

• To what extent do adults engage sensitively with children's play? How can you support and extend the themes of children's play, building tomorrow on what happened today?

• Can you deepen your understanding of play through further study, observation and reflection? How can you share your insights with parents and the wider community in meaningful ways?

4 An environment for living and learning

A Froebelian environment reflects a view of children as active, creative, social learners. Froebelian environments may look very different, but they will be underpinned by the same guiding principles. A Froebelian environment is not excessively neat, ordered and quiet. Nor is it excessively messy, chaotic or noisy. Instead, it unites elements of order and chaos, calmness and exuberance, predictability and surprise, flexibility and routine, planning and spontaneity. All, in their different ways, contribute to a dynamic learning environment which can be shaped by children and adults.

Too often children are given a pre-packaged, 'out of a catalogue', plasticised environment which can be bland, static and sterile. Routines can sometimes be so rigid that children are hurried and harried from one event to the next. Learning in such environments becomes responsive and passive rather than creative and active.

A Froebelian environment, in contrast, is creative and open-ended and it includes a balance of bought and found materials, made and natural. It is based on respect, trust, warm responsive relationships and rich first-hand and play experience. The environment is seen as flexible, transformable and responsive to children's changing interests and preoccupations.

Figure 4.1 A flexible environment which is responsive to changing interests. Here the children have been exploring the flow of water through tubes.

Key principles underpinning a Froebelian environment

These are some of the principles which underpin a Froebelian environment for young children:

- indoors and outdoors
- rich first-hand experience
- free choice and movement
- connectedness
- independence and interdependence
- time for play
- warm, responsive, interesting, trusting relationships
- a place where individuals feel significant in the whole community.

Indoors and outdoors

The indoors and outdoors are viewed as integral parts of one whole environment, and both have equal value. Wherever possible, children can move easily between indoors and outdoors, and play can flow without interruption. The boundary between outdoors and indoors is therefore blurred and space is seen as an interconnected whole.

Rich first-hand experience

A Froebelian environment provides a rich array of genuine 'real world' experiences which offer exciting opportunities for learning and which engage children's interests. Experiences such as digging the vegetable plot, churning butter, making apple juice, popping corn, meeting new people with particular skills and enthusiasms, visiting a local heliport, rolling in autumn leaves, and paddling in streams are just a few examples. Such experiences broaden children's understanding and confirm the world as a source of beauty, mystery and wonder.

Alongside such new experiences children take part in the everyday life of the early years setting, making the snacks, setting the table for dinner, washing the paint pots, watering the plants, oiling the wheels on the bikes, and so on. These everyday routines are significant learning experiences, but all too often are carried out by adults alone. Setting the table for dinner, for example, involves children in counting chairs, cutlery and cups, reading name cards, thinking about concepts of 'next to' and 'opposite', filling and carrying jugs of water, and so on. Froebel emphasised that children's involvement in everyday tasks was an important way that they could learn alongside adults. Contributing to the life of the community was also an important part of belonging to it. The Early Years Foundation Stage states 'children learn by doing things and doing things with other people who are more competent, rather than just being told' (DCSF 2008).

Free choice and movement

For most of the day children have free choice from a range of different resources and experiences many of which have their origins in Froebel's 'gifts and occupations' (see Chapter 5). Core areas of experience are available on a daily basis, and most are provided indoors and outdoors. These experiences are carefully planned to encourage children to make links and connections between them. Core experiences include:

blocks	literature, books and stories
sand and water	role play
construction, modelling and making	woodwork
	small world play
clay and other malleable materials	music, movement and dance
	investigative areas
painting, printing and colour mixing	mark-making, drawing, writing and book-making

Settings for the youngest children include treasure baskets and heuristic play resources and settings for children over 2 may include cooking, sewing and ICT areas. (See, for example, *Core Experiences in the Early Years Foundation Stage* (2009) produced by the Kate Greenaway Nursery School and Children's Centre.)

Core experiences are carefully planned to promote learning in all areas of the curriculum and to support children in using the resources in increasingly complex ways.

Connectedness

'Connectedness' is a key Froebelian principle. Froebel argued that making connections is fundamental to learning as children link different domains of experience and make sense of the new in relation to what is already known.

Research by Chris Athey (2007) and the Froebel Early Education Project has confirmed the importance of children making cognitive connections between features of their environment. Research in the neurosciences also confirms how rich and varied activity and experience builds connections in the brain.

A Froebelian approach encourages and supports children to make connections between different areas of the environment, between resources and fundamentally between ideas. This means a fluid, flexible environment where play and activity can flow easily from one area to another and where children are encouraged to combine materials where appropriate, and to pursue their ideas through different media. This important principle of 'connectedness' can be seen in the following example.

Two 4-year-old boys made a robot with recycled materials in the workshop area. They wanted the robot to have flashing eyes so they moved to the investigative area where they found batteries, crocodile clips and light bulbs. Using their previous knowledge of these materials and a small amount of adult help they succeeded in lighting up the robot's eyes.

Here, the children's learning is extended as they make connections between different areas of provision and between ideas. Of crucial importance is the adult support and encouragement to make such links. Allowing such connections does not lead to chaos. Children are very willing to accept reasonable limitations (for example, that jigsaw pieces are not used for mixing in the sand) if there are plenty of ready alternatives.

Independence and interdependence

Froebel emphasised the importance of children doing things for themselves as well as doing things together. He observed how children actively seek out obstacles and enjoy overcoming them and he argued that we underestimate children's abilities and their delight in new achievements. He gives an example of a young child climbing over a log blocking a pathway:

'Let it alone', he will cry as his father goes to take a log out of his way, 'I'll get over it'. When he gets over it by himself, however difficult it may be, he is encouraged by the success and goes back to climb it again; soon he is jumping over it as if there were nothing in his way.

(Froebel, in Lilley 1967: 125)

A Froebelian environment is carefully planned to ensure that children can be autonomous in choosing, selecting and using the resources, either alone or with others. Materials are carefully organised in open-access storage. This ensures that children make decisions about what they need for a particular purpose.

As Froebel emphasised, the freedom to make choices brings responsibility in both how the material is used and the need to return it, even if this is done collectively in a fun activity at the end of the session. Materials are of good quality and well presented so that children are encouraged to value them. Appropriate mess is an acceptable part of the play environment but mops, cloths, brushes and brooms are available so that children can take increasing responsibility for clearing up and restoring a sense of order to the environment.

Independent cooking

Some Froebelian settings include a cooking area which is carefully planned to support children in cooking on their own or with others. The child in Figure 4.2 is making her own chocolate crispies. She selects the recipe book, assembles the utensils she needs, counts the necessary spoonfuls of raw ingredients and grates the chocolate. Then, with minimal adult assistance, she melts the chocolate over a candle 'food warmer' and mixes the ingredients. She carefully writes her name on the paper cases, spoons in the mixture, leaves the crispies to harden while she washes the utensils in a nearby sink. Finally she shares her crispies with her friend, turning an individual activity into a social act of friendship.

In this simple cooking activity, she is involved in reading, writing and counting. She experiences first-hand the effect of heat on solid

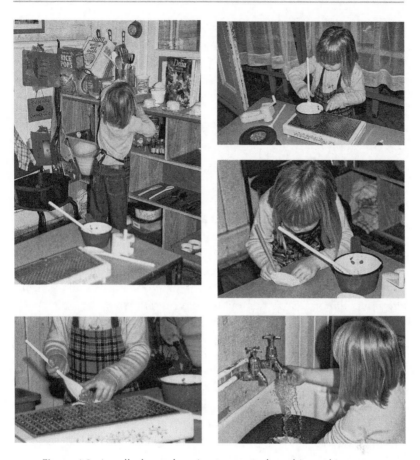

Figure 4.2 A well-planned environment, such as this cooking area, supports autonomous learning.

chocolate and how liquid chocolate turns back to solid as it cools. She is developing fine manipulative skills as well as considerable self-confidence and a feeling of self-efficacy. She learns how to assess possible danger, to manage risk and take responsibility for her own actions. All these are combined in a freely chosen self-activity which makes sense and is meaningful to her.

As children develop skill and confidence they can master more complicated recipes, including baking a cake on their birthday to share with others. Underpinning this experience are some key Froebelian principles:

- the importance of a well-planned environment to enable children's autonomy
- appropriately high expectations of what children can do, given a supportive environment
- freedom and responsibility
- trust in children's growing competence
- an integrated curriculum where all areas of learning come together in a meaningful whole.

However, although children learn by doing things on their own they also learn with and through others. The environment also allows children to collaborate together and to help each other.

Time which enables rather than constrains

The way time is organised can inhibit as well as enable children's learning. For example, when time is broken up so that children are moved from one activity to another, this can lead to a lack of concentration and persistence and superficial, disconnected learning.

Froebelian educators create long periods of open-ended, uninterrupted time so that both children and adults can become deeply involved in play and other learning activities. Time is not 'filled' but is freed from all unnecessary interruptions.

The use of adults' time is crucially linked to children's growing independence and autonomy. The more children are able to do things for themselves and manage their environment themselves, the more adults have time to engage in worthwhile conversation, develop close relationships and observe and extend children's learning. The availability of time is therefore a key feature of a Froebelian environment.

Figure 4.3 Positive relationships – sharing delight in operating the pulley.

Warm, responsive, interesting, trusting relationships

Although the physical features of the environment are important, it is relationships with adults and other children which are crucial. Peter Elfer, Principal Lecturer at Froebel College, University of Roehampton, makes a powerful case for emotional and interpersonal connectedness. Adults need to develop a genuine bond with the child and child's family and build relationships which are close, responsive, tuned in and consistent. He emphasises the importance of seeing children as active learners with autonomy and agency but at the same time holding their more dependent and vulnerable sides in mind. A 'key person approach' is an important way that individual children can establish close relationships with adults within an early years setting and can feel they are significant and thought about in the whole community (Elfer *et al.* 2011). Dorothy Selleck gives an example of such a sensitive approach:

> Joshua took in a magnificent marrow from the family allotment to his nursery. His key person, Clare, listened to Joshua and his mum as he eased gently back into the bustle and the anticipation of a day with friends. After repeated hugs and kisses for his mum and baby brother, Joshua let go and was off and away. At the end of the day, we found that the marrow had been weighed, measured and cut up. Many little fingers had explored its viscous flesh and the seeds were saved up for planting in the EYFS outdoor learning area. One half had been hollowed out and hung up on a tree as a bird feeder and rings of the fruit had been used for printing.
>
> I hope more children and their families more of the time will be in special relationships with their key person, so that their home culture (allotments) vulnerabilities (separating) and enthusiasms (growing food) can be shared.
>
> (Selleck 2009: 5)

A place where individuals feel significant in a whole community

This is a key Froebelian principle. Froebel believed that each individual child is unique but gains in significance as part of a whole supportive and loving community.

Froebel saw play, ring games, stories, singing, dancing and the cele-bration of festivals as important ways of creating a sense of community. Play and storytelling are also significant ways that children build friendships and inclusive communities. Gussin Paley (2010) argues that fantasy play can provide the glue that binds the community together and provides the nourishment for cognitive, narrative and social connectivity.

When each child feels thought about, listened to and respected, and where they feel connected to, not isolated from their own family life and culture, then positive relationships and friendships can flourish.

Conclusion

This chapter has looked at just some features of a Froebelian environ-ment. Underpinning these features are key Froebelian principles of respect for children's developing autonomy and competence, the significance of positive, enabling relationships, and the importance of a strong, cohesive community where individuals can flourish (Froebel's idea of 'unity in diversity'). The principle of connectedness and links between areas and ideas are fundamental to a Froebelian approach. Further aspects of the environment, the resources and the garden are considered in the next two chapters.

Bringing the Froebel approach to your environment

- Does the environment you offer support children in being active, curious, investigative, autonomous, creative, imaginative and social learners?

- Does the environment support or inhibit children in making connections?

- How flexible is the environment? Is it responsive to children's changing interests and enthusiasms? Can they transform the environment for their own purposes?

- Reflect on the example of a 'cooking area'. Do we sometimes underestimate what children can do themselves, given appropriate support?

- Reflect on how time is organised in your setting. Why do you think it is organised this way? Is there sufficient time for extended involvement in self-chosen activity?

- Are the indoor and outdoor environment seen as one whole learning environment? Do you think the outdoors is valued as much as the indoor area? In all weathers?

5 | Resources and how they are used

Froebel's 'gifts and occupations'

Froebel devised a series of simple but carefully planned materials he called 'gifts and occcupations' for use in his kindergartens. These, together with nature, stories, movement games, music, songs and rhymes, were integral to his educational approach. However, it was not just the resources but the ideas underpinning them that were important to Froebel. Materials on their own were not enough. Adults had to engage with and understand the processes of development in the child.

The gifts

The first gift was a soft ball on a piece of string, for babies and very young children to play with. It was designed to be able to be reached for, grasped and held in the hand. The baby could roll it, push it and swing it back and forth. Inevitably the ball would roll away, and awareness of lost and found, disappearance and appearance could be fostered. Adults could play hide and seek or pretend the ball was, say, a cat – and make it jump. Later a set of eight different coloured balls was introduced. Froebel collected over fifty different ways of playing with the balls, based on his observations of how children used them.

The second gift (Figure 5.1) consisted of a wooden sphere, cube and cylinder, providing a contrast with the soft ball. The shapes have different characteristics: the sphere rolls but the cube stays put or slides. However the cylinder combines elements of both, and it can roll and slide. The cube, which had a hole through the middle, could be spun fast on a stick, creating the appearance of the cylinder. This gift, Froebel argued, helped very young children to begin to understand about similarities and opposites, unity and diversity. The law of opposites was an important educational principle for Froebel. New experience challenges what is known and new connections have to be built with existing understandings. We can also deepen our understanding of something by knowing about its opposite.

The third gift was a small box consisting of a wooden cube sub-divided into eight smaller cubes, intended particularly for children aged 1 to 3. Froebel recognised young children's fascination with taking things apart and re-assembling them, and play with the blocks enabled a child to do this. Gifts four, five (Figure 5.2) and six were similar boxed sets of blocks, divided in varied ways to create different geometric shapes, but with all the parts forming a whole cube. This wholeness or unity was a key principle for Froebel.

Figure 5.1 Froebel's second gift.

Figure 5.2 Froebel's fifth gift.

These small wooden blocks were for children to play with, to represent things from their own experience, create stories, or make beautiful patterns as well as to begin to understand geometric relationships. The gifts could also foster a close relationship between child and adult as they played together (Liebschner 1992).

Today we can find Froebel's gifts in the wooden hollow and unit blocks which are larger in size but reflect similar mathematically precise forms (see Chapter 8).

The occupations

Froebel devised a wide range of materials and activities for children in his kindergartens, many of which can still be seen in early years settings today. Froebel did not see these as separate activities, however, but as connected parts of a whole approach. Froebel's occupations included:

- painting and drawing
- threads and punched cards for sewing
- paper pricking (making pictures and patterns by pricking holes in a piece of paper and holding it against the light)
- paper cutting, weaving and paper folding (similar to origami)
- sticks for arranging in patterns and shapes.
- wooden shapes for parquetry-type pattern-making
- peas and sticks for construction (similar to construction kits today)
- clay and wax for modelling
- potatoes, turnip stalks and soft wood for cutting and shaping
- sand and stones.

The occupations were particularly important for developing an understanding of two- and three-dimensional materials, for solving problems and developing physical skills, and for representing, expressing, communicating and being creative. Froebel described the resources for children to create within his own kindergarten:

> First there is plastic material – soft clay, wet sand, water, and air to drive and turn things. Second there are less solid objects such as small flat pieces of wood, smooth paper, or sticks and threads. Last, there is a choice of dry sand, sawdust, glass which can be moistened and breathed on, and objects such as slates, slate pencils, paper, chalk or crayons.
>
> So the child takes pleasure in painting and drawing, and both are essential for his education. Music is especially important, since the sounds which he produces in singing or by striking bells or glass or metal serve to give creative expression to feelings and ideas.
>
> (Froebel, in Lilley 1967: 113)

Resources then were simple (but based on complex ideas) and open-ended, offering a wide variety of different creative possibilities. Children could elaborate their ideas with increasing complexity as they gained more experience and understanding. Crucially, they were seen as inter-connected parts of a whole approach, not as separate 'activities'.

In Froebel's gifts and occupations can be seen the origins of many of the resources offered in early years settings today. However, the same resources can be used in many different ways. The underpinning principles are therefore essential.

Resources today

Heuristic play resources for babies and toddlers

Elinor Goldschmied, a Froebel-trained teacher and later social worker, who devoted much of her life to improving provision for babies and toddlers in particular, highlighted the importance of heuristic play materials for very young children in nursery settings. Rather than plastic toys which have a limited range of possibilities she argued for the provision of beautiful, interesting, sensory-rich objects which offer end-less possibilities and combinations. Resources include such things as tins, pegs, small balls, wooden pegs, pebbles, fir cones, shells, ribbons and much more, carefully stored in drawstring bags. The materials are intended to promote exploration, investigation, problem solving and discovery, and focused, concentrated attention. The adult has a key role in preparing the materials and then offering a calm, attentive presence and 'emotional anchorage' rather than intervening or leading the play.

She also devised 'treasure baskets' of beautifully textured, fascinating objects that would offer rich sensory experiences and body movement for babies who are sitting up (Figure 5.3). Goldschmied argued that 'we pay attention to [a child's] diet but what about her mental diet which nurtures her developing capacity to use eyes, hand and mouth in concentrated activity' (Goldschmied and Jackson 1994: 88).

Heuristic play and treasure basket materials illustrate some impor-tant Froebelian principles about resources:

Figure 5.3 Exploring 'everyday' objects in a treasure basket.

- the value of simple, open-ended, flexible materials which can be combined in many different ways, creating new possibilities
- carefully thought about, aesthetically pleasing materials which offer rich sensory stimulation
- use of 'everyday' materials which can be adapted to any home or group situation
- free choice and self-activity – the child as an active learner.

Things to take apart and investigate

Froebel recognised the almost universal desire of small children to take things apart and investigate them. Children are curious about how things work as well as what they do. Taking things apart helps children to see how the component parts contribute to the whole, a key Froebelian concept.

Figure 5.4 Investigating how
and why things work.

A Froebelian setting includes a plentiful supply of things to operate and investigate, including water wheels, large-scale water pumps, pulley wheels for lifting sand or transporting water, pottery wheels, old mincers and much more. A box with a selection of old clocks, plugs, radios and such like, together with a selection of screwdrivers, encourages extended periods of 'tinkering' as children concentrate hard on opening things up and seeing what is inside. I remember children spending hours with an old butter churn I found in a charity shop. They were fascinated to explore cause and effect and find that turning the handle made the small cogwheel turn – which made the large cogwheel turn – which made the whisk rotate in the milk – and produced butter at the end of the process!

It is interesting to note that one of the largest aerospace research companies in the USA asks its potential recruits at interview about their childhood experience of this type of investigative play. They found that engineers with such experience could toss a problem around, break it down, tease out its critical elements and rearrange them in innovate ways that led to a solution, whereas many highly qualified graduates without such childhood play experience could not (Brown 2009: 8).

Open-ended resources

A Froebel approach provides a wide range of open-ended resources such as blocks, sand, water, clay, recycled materials, graphics materials, paint, and so on. They are 'open-ended' in that there is no fixed, required ways of using them – instead there are many possibilities (Bruce *et al.* 2008). Open-ended materials can promote discovery, inventiveness, creativity and imagination. For example, resources such as large blocks, crates, planks and wheels can be a fire engine one day and a car or train another day. They can be whatever children want them to be. They are flexible and responsive to children's changing interests. This ability to transform objects is hugely significant in young children's learning as it develops fluency in using symbols and abstract ideas.

Similarly, resources for imaginative and role play, including 'home play' areas, include many open-ended resources such as blankets, boxes, den-type structures, fabrics, simple multipurpose dressing-up clothes and furniture which can easily be adapted for a sink, washing machine, cooker, fridge, bed or cot. Some replica material, for example a toy iron, is supportive for younger or less experienced children to enter into the world of pretence, but increasingly they will find their own resources, such as a block to use as an iron. The simpler the resources, the more complex the play, the more varied the play themes and the more complex the interaction as children have to negotiate their ideas together.

Froebelian settings therefore avoid the vast array of commercial, usually plastic, replica play resources which are so often marketed as 'educational'. There are no 'pre-packaged' play scenarios set up by adults as part of the 'theme of the week'. Instead, children are helped to develop their own play themes with supportive and imaginative adults and these might continue and evolve for as long as the interest lasts. In this way children develop inner resources they can use over and over again.

Multi-purpose workshop areas

These workshop areas allow children to select the resources they need for a particular purpose. For example, a 'making' workshop area includes a wide range of recycled and craft resources, glues, tapes, staplers, pens, paints, printing materials, and so on. It is a very dynamic place and will change from day to day, even from hour to hour. Many children use the workshop area to make props for their play, for example watches, magic wands, mobile phones, superhero capes, headbands, crowns, and so on. The workshop area also allows children to draw, cut out and animate their drawings, bringing them to life.

For example, in Figure 5.5 the boy below drew faces on pieces of card. He then rolled up the cards to make puppets, attaching straws for legs and arms. He struggled to attach a piece of wool to one puppet and joined straws to attach to another. The resulting puppets represented Little Red Riding Hood, the wolf, complete with tail, and a hunter with a gun to shoot the wolf. He demonstrated his creativity, persistence and ability to solve problems, and at the same time he entered into an imaginary world, making a familiar story come alive.

A Froebelian approach seeks to develop children's creativity and imagination. It does not use templates, cut-outs, stencils or any pre-drawn outlines. There will be no screwed-up tissue paper for children to stick on an adult's pre-drawn outline. Nor will there be mass-produced factory-style products designed by adults but assembled by children. Instead adults support children in using their own ideas to make their own representations in their own way, individually or collaboratively. Children sometimes need help in pursuing their ideas and adults will offer support or introduce techniques at the time they

Figure 5.5 A workshop area with open-access materials.

are needed. In this way children build up considerable technical competence which they can draw on in new, more complex ways.

Woodwork

A woodwork workshop area, indoors or outdoors is an everyday resource in a Froebelian setting for children over 3. Children have access to saws, hammers, nails, screwdrivers and screws, and a child-height woodwork bench with a vice to hold the wood stable and a plentiful supply of offcuts of soft wood. Accessories such as bottle tops, cotton reels and cardboard wheels are added. The woodwork area is carefully planned so that all the tools have their own storage space and can be found and returned safely. Clear rules are established and safe use of the tools is taught.

Children might start off hammering nails or sawing wood for the sake of it, practising the skills of using the tools. As they develop more competence they begin to join and connect pieces of wood, and saw wood for a particular purpose. They are involved in problem solving, estimating, measuring, and talk about how the wood is too long, too short, too thick, and so on. The woodwork bench is rich in potential for creativity, problem solving, reasoning and numeracy, as well as physical coordination, social responsibility and learning how to manage risk safely (Figure 5.6).

Clay

Clay is very responsive to small hands (Figure 5.7). It can be pummelled, poked, pinched, squeezed, flattened and rolled – and it always holds its shape. It offers endless possibilities for moulding, pattern making and representing whatever the child wants it to be. Water can be added, making it deliciously sloppy and sloshy.

Lucy Parker, a Froebelian teacher, observed children's use of clay as part of her Masters research. She found that the open-ended nature of the material allowed children to use it as a symbolic language in highly

Figure 5.6 A woodwork bench provides experience in using real tools.

creative and imaginative ways. Using the clay outdoors, when the weather was suitable, extended the representational experience. Children collected flowers, grass seeds, berries and leaves and incorporated them into their creations. Flowers became treasure and cake decorations, stones became candles, and berries became crocodile eyes. New connections opened up in meaningful ways and added to children's creativity and imagination (Parker 2006).

Natural materials

A Froebelian setting includes many natural resources such as stones, pebbles, shells, cones, feathers, petals, leaves, straw, sticks, dried seeds and seed heads which are selected for their interesting textures, shapes and tones. Children use them for making patterns and pictures and they can be rearranged in many different ways. The child in Figure 5.8 is

Figure 5.7 Clay offers endless possibilities for moulding and creating.

Figure 5.8 Creating patterns, using pebbles, stones and sticks.

using polished pebbles, stones and thin sticks from the garden to create pictures and patterns. He is exploring space, lines, patterns, enclosures, similarities and differences. He is matching, sorting, ordering and counting. He can reshape his designs as he wishes.

Sand and water

Sand and water are timeless play materials, introduced in Froebel's kindergarten 170 years ago and available in most early years settings today. Sand and water are offered separately and combined, indoors and outdoors, in large trays but also, where possible, in large sand and water areas where they can be mixed and combined together.

Sand and water offer much potential as materials to be explored but they can also be transformed into imaginative play scenarios. The sand area might be a place for digging water channels for boats, burying treasure or operating pulleys. The water area might include pipes, tubes and gutters, waterwheels and pumps, or it might be a place for making pretend soup, or a scenario for imaginative narratives about swimming and drowning. The essential thing is that the resources are responsive to children's ideas, interests and preoccupations and that children can be autonomous in selecting, within reason, the materials they want. Adults can then tune into and engage with children's intentions.

Books and stories, graphic areas, book-making, drawing and writing

Stories are central to a Froebelian setting. They provide a rich, shared culture of imagined and real narratives which all children can draw on in their play. Children make stories everywhere, with natural materials, small worlds, blocks, sand and water, and much more. These are often written down and made into books. A quiet, warm and comfortable area for sharing books together is available indoors and outdoors but books will also be available in all key areas – for example, recipe books in the cooking area, finding-out books in the investigative area, art books in the workshop areas, music and song books in the music area, books about buildings and constructions in the block area, and so on.

A graphics area provides tools for drawing and writing, carefully organised and easily accessible. Paper, card and staplers are available for making books, and adults work with children to help them develop their own ideas. The children in Figure 5.9 are making zig-zag books about the recent hatching of the chicks. They are building on their first-hand experience and using what they know about writing and drawing to communicate their ideas in a context which makes sense.

Music and dance

A quiet music area with beautiful sound-making resources and a variety of instruments – bought, found, made and recycled – is freely available in a Froebelian setting. Children can explore sounds, engage in rhythmic 'conversations' with adults and other children and compose their own dances, indoors and outdoors. They can make connections with

Figure 5.9 Resources for drawing, writing and book-making.

Figure 5.10 An area for exploring sound and creating music.

the music and dance of their own cultural traditions as well as creating and sharing new interpretations.

Conclusion

This chapter has looked at some of the key resources in an early years setting. However no particular resources are valuable in themselves – it is what children and adults do with them that is important. Resources are just tools for thinking, representing and communicating, and children see play potential in materials which we may not anticipate. Learning is a social process and children learn with and through others. The richest resources of all are therefore the other children and the adults in the setting.

Bringing a Froebel approach to early years resources

- Are there sufficient open-ended resources offering multiple possibilities for play and exploration?

- Think about Froebel's 'gifts and occupations'. What links can you make with resources in early years settings today?

- Could you involve parents and friends in collecting everyday items for children to take apart and investigate?

- How might children be supported in using wood, stones, clay, sticks and other natural materials in creative and imaginative ways?

6 | The nursery garden and play outdoors

The garden is the essence of a Froebelian early years setting. It offers space to move freely and expansively, to run, leap and frolic, and to play with abandon. The outdoors provides direct contact with nature which can stimulate all the senses and provoke wonder, curiosity and exploration. It is a dynamic environment which is always full of surprise, and children can shape and transform it for their own purposes. Outdoors is a place for moving, thinking, feeling, imagining and creating.

A Froebelian garden is seen as a rich learning environment which can complement and link with the indoor area but which also offers unique learning experiences which cannot be provided indoors. Although carefully thought about by adults, it offers a child's domain where children have more freedom and space to initiate and sustain their own play themes. In particular the outdoor area offers:

- engagement with the natural world

- space and freedom for whole body, expansive movement

- opportunities for adventure, risk and challenge

- a flexible context for imaginative play and creative thinking

- meaningful learning in all areas of the curriculum.

A Froebelian garden is not seen as a 'playtime' area but is available throughout the day, so that wherever possible children have free movement between the indoor and outdoor space. Weather conditions such as snow, ice, rain and wind are seen as fascinating and fun learning experiences, not as reasons to stay indoors.

Engagement with the natural world

Direct experience of nature was essential to Froebel. Children learnt *in* nature rather than just *about* nature. Through gardening and play outdoors children were immersed in the natural world and could learn about the growth of plants and animals, about the beauty of nature and about the interrelationships of all living things. They also learnt to care for and take responsibility for nature and gradually to develop a sense of personal responsibility.

> The child who has cared for another living thing . . . is more easily led to care for his own life. The care of plants will also satisfy his desire to watch living creatures, for he will see birds and butterflies and beetles coming nearby.
>
> (Froebel, in Lilley 1967: 128)

Through gardening, children experience the cycles of life and death, growth and decay, recycling and conserving resources in direct and meaningful ways.

Today, as children spend longer amounts of time indoors and are increasingly disconnected from the natural world, Froebel's ideas have renewed importance and urgency. If children can develop a sense of wonder about nature, can see the effect of their actions on things around them and can get to know their own small garden in deep ways, they are much more likely to want to help shape a sustainable future.

A Froebelian garden is therefore planned to include trees, bushes, and wild and cultivated areas. There are gardens where children can grow flowers, fruit, vegetables, herbs and spices as well as a digging patch where they can investigate the soil, making fascinating discoveries. Ideally, there are wild areas where children can experience the excitement of hiding in and navigating through tangled plants and

Figure 6.1 Finding and observing small creatures outdoors.

tall grass. There are numerous habitats for wildlife, such as stones and rotting logs, ponds, nesting boxes, and so on. Where space is limited then growing potatoes in tubs, or using an old sink as a pond, provides at least some contact with nature on a smaller scale.

Nature can be provocative and at times challenging, and children can be fascinated by the rawness as well as the beauty of nature. I remember children being transfixed when they found a dead bird in the garden – and question followed question. A Froebelian approach does not shy away from difficult subjects but recognises children's fascination with natural processes.

Earth, fire, air and water

Earth, fire, air and water are elemental materials which provide multiple learning opportunities outdoors. Earth is explored through digging, planting, composting, and so on. Resources such as hosepipes, water

Figure 6.2 Digging the soil before planting seeds in the garden.

pumps, waterwheels, gutters and pipes enable children to explore water and how it flows. For example, the waterwheel in Figure 6.3 provides experience of the force of water and the relationship between the flow of water and the rotation of the wheel. Children begin to see a connection between the gradient of the slope, the speed of the water and the movement of the wheel. Similarly the movement of air can be explored through hand and foot pumps or through windmills, kites, and so on.

Fire might be more controversial, yet many Froebelian early years settings include fire as a key experience outdoors. Fire is an exciting sensory experience. The smell and sound of burning wood, the movement of the flames, and the feel of the heat can captivate both children and adults alike. Building and then cooking on a fire can be a rich learning experience as well as an important social and communal event. The effect of water on fire can be experienced, as well as the difference between smoke and steam. Through fire, children can experience and learn about:

Figure 6.3 Exploring the effect of water on the wheel.

- things that burn and things that melt

- how heat changes materials

- the difference between steam and smoke

- new words in a meaningful context such as spark, crackle, b ...s, billowing

- how charcoal is made and how it can be collected and used for drawing

- the effect of water and air on fire

- the potential danger of fire and how to manage it safely.

Clearly, creating an area for a fire and managing it with groups of children involves careful organisation and planning, as well as discussion with parents. It is not something to be introduced when there are new children in the group or shortages of staff. In my experience, however, sitting round a fire on a cold winter's day, cooking soup and having endless conversations is one of the richest learning experiences with young children that I can remember.

Space and freedom for whole-body, expansive movement

Movement is essential for growing brains and bodies. Froebel emphasised the connections between movement, thought and feeling. Today, work in the neurosciences supports the connections between the body, brain and mind, and emphasises the links between action and conceptual thought (Athey 2007). For example, moving headfirst down a slide offers experience of such things as direction, gradient and speed and the concepts of 'headfirst' or even 'headfirst backwards'. Climbing offers whole-body experience of moving up, down, over, under, through, in between and on top of, as well as concepts of height and balance. Swinging on a rope can provide experience of concepts such as energy, forces, gravity, speed, distance, cause and effect.

Figure 6.4 Challenging opportunities for moving in space.

Research on developmental-movement play shows the importance of a wide variety of movements, such as tipping, tumbling, rolling, scrambling and swinging, in developing a sense of balance and a sense of one's own body in space. Such movements can have a significant impact on children's later learning (Greenland 2006). Research in Norway by Ingunn Fjortoft (2004) has shown the importance of rough ground, uneven surfaces and wild areas in enhancing the physical fitness of children as well as their sustained, imaginative, collaborative play.

A Froebelian outdoor area is therefore carefully planned to provide a wide range of opportunities for movement, including swinging, sliding, balancing, crawling and climbing, so that children can move their bodies in space. Resources are flexible enough to ensure challenge for the most timid and the most adventurous. For example, one Froebelian setting positioned an enclosed fabric rope swing over a sand pit. The toddlers enjoyed twisting the rope, resulting in rapidly rotating movements as the rope unwound. This was an exhilarating, exciting experience of spinning – and the sand provided a soft landing for any falls.

Opportunities for adventure, risk and challenge

The rope example above might appear 'too risky' for some practitioners. However, a Froebelian approach includes many opportunities for positive risk taking and adventurous play outdoors. Children are often drawn to activities they perceive to be 'scary', such as sliding fast, hanging upside down or balancing on a rickety bridge. No sooner have they mastered something than they practise it, vary it and add extra challenges – like moving down a slide headfirst, or even headfirst backwards.

Such adventurous play allows them to become confident and capable, to test their limits and to find out how their bodies work in space. Risk is part of life and children need to be exposed to appropriate levels of risk in order to learn how to manage it and develop the skills to be safe. The English Early Years Foundation Stage guidance (DCSF 2008) emphasises the importance of 'reasonable risk taking' and

states that adults should 'build children's confidence to take manage-
able risks in their play'.

Froebel made much the same point when he discussed the issue of
tree climbing:

> To climb a new tree is . . . to discover a new world; seen from above,
> everything looks quite different from the usual telescoped, distorted
> side-view. If we could remember our joy when in childhood we
> looked out beyond the cramping limits of our immediate surround-
> ings, we should not be so insensitive to call out, 'Come down, you
> will fall'. One learns to protect oneself from falling by looking over
> and around a place as well as by physical movement, and the most
> ordinary thing certainly looks quite different from above.
>
> 'But he will be reckless and I shall never be free of anxiety about
> him.'
>
> No, the boy whose training has always been connected with the
> gradual development of his capacities will attempt only a little more
> than he has already been able to do, and will come safely through
> all these dangers. It is the boy who does not know his strength and
> the demands made on it who is likely to venture beyond his experi-
> ence and run into unsuspected danger.
>
> (Froebel, in Lilley 1967: 126)

Here Froebel focused on the benefits rather than the risks of climbing
trees. He recognised the sense of joy and freedom associated with
pushing the boundaries beyond the limits of everyday experience and
the opportunities to learn about such things as height and perspective.
Children can find out how their bodies work in a challenging context
by testing their nerve, strength and skill. Physical, cognitive, personal
and emotional learning are integrated in one activity.

Froebel also argued that children who experience increasing
challenges in play are safer than children who have been protected
from them. He shows a view of children as adventure-seekers, looking
for new challenges and problems to overcome, and of adults who need
to be supportive of this sense of adventure rather than undermining
it with negative comments such as 'Come down – you'll fall'. The Early

Figure 6.5 'To climb a tree is to discover a new world' (Froebel).

Years Foundation Stage guidance makes much the same point. 'Being over-protected can prevent children from learning about possible dangers and about how to protect themselves from harm' (DCSF 2008).

A Froebelian setting includes many resources that promote adventurous play and allow children to have experiences that they find challenging but which do not expose them to unnecessary danger. This might include trees and ladders to climb, ropes to swing on, bars to hang upside down from and resources which offer challenge to the confident as well as the more hesitant child.

However, it is the adults' attitudes, not just the resources, which make the biggest difference in satisfying children's hunger for physical challenge (Stephenson 2003). In a Froebelian approach, adults enjoy being outside, recognise the importance of physical challenge and know individual children's capabilities. They support children to assess risks for themselves and to learn the necessary skills to be safe. When adults show a positive attitude to challenge, seeing it as something to be relished rather than feared, and celebrate achievements, however small, children are more likely to develop self-confidence, the willingness to 'have a go' and the persistence to keep on trying, which are all important learning dispositions.

A flexible context for imaginative play and creative thinking

Imagination and pretence thrive in the more open-ended nature of the outdoor space. Much of children's imaginative play involves movement – for example, going on holiday, delivering things, rescuing people, chasing robbers, transporting people to hospital, and so on. A Froebelian outdoor setting includes many opportunities for these play themes to flourish. It is not filled with fixed, pre-designed equipment such as trains, space rockets and castles. Rather it includes interesting spaces and open-ended materials for children to create their own trains, space rockets and castles – or anything else they want to create. With a plentiful supply of play props and 'loose parts' such as crates, blankets, boxes, ladders, wheels and planks, as well as support from

Figure 6.6 Creating imaginary worlds in small enclosed spaces.

adults who value such play, children can create their own imaginary worlds.

Froebel noted how children liked to create their own worlds in small secret spaces such as a corner of a garden, shed or box and that, if space permitted, children would often work collaboratively to construct their own dens (Froebel, in Lilley 1967: 128). Such secret spaces are important ways in which children feel a sense of agency in shaping their own imaginary worlds.

A Froebelian setting includes spaces for children to create their own worlds. For example the bushes shown in Figure 6.6 were planted in a circle to create an enclosed space. Here children could create their own play scenarios, using available material such as leaves, twigs and stones as props. Such play requires higher-level thinking as objects are transformed symbolically and children have to negotiate their meaning at an abstract level.

Meaningful learning in all areas of the curriculum

Observing insects under logs, seeing how long the ice takes to melt, watering the garden with a hose, building with large recycled boxes, digging for ancient treasure, drawing treasure maps, writing tickets for a pretend train, or acting out a well-loved story, are just some examples of mathematical, scientific, musical, historical, geographical, technological and literacy learning. Froebelian educators recognise these emerging subject areas in children's learning, but in practice they are experienced by children as a meaningful whole.

For example, the children in Figure 6.7 made sandwiches, using tomatoes grown in the garden. They sliced the tomatoes, talked about the seeds inside and noticed the smell of the freshly picked tomatoes. They spread butter on slices of bread, made sandwiches, cut them in half, changing the shape from square to rectangle, then in half again, changing to square again. Some were cut diagonally into triangles. Halves and quarters were discussed in meaningful ways. The sandwiches were put on a plate to be shared with others for snacks. There were books about growing tomatoes and the adult made up a song about 'sandwich on my plate, sandwich on my plate, yummy, yummy, yummy, yummy, sandwich on my plate'. Children and adults added new verses such as 'tomatoes on the bush', or 'sandwich in my tum', and so on.

Photos recorded the process – from when children planted the tomatoes to harvesting, to sandwich-making – and were made into a visual presentation for sharing with parents and later a book. Here all the areas of learning come together in one coherent 'whole' experience.

Conclusion

Froebel's emphasis on the garden as a spiritual place of beauty and harmony, where children can develop respect for and responsibility for nature, has increasing urgency today as so many children grow up surrounded by concrete. His ideas of freedom and responsibility, individual and community, and learning with and through others in a rich outdoor environment still resonate today. The use of the outdoors

Figure 6.7 Making sandwiches from tomatoes grown in the garden.

as a unique learning environment, linked to the indoor area, is central to a Froebelian approach but one which requires considerable thought and planning if its potential is ever to be realised.

Bringing the Froebel approach to your garden and outdoor play

* Are there opportunities for children to play adventurously outdoors? Can they push their own limits and do things which are enjoyably 'scary'?

* Do children have the 'support of attentive and engaged adults who are enthusiastic about the outdoors and understand the importance of outdoor learning' (DCSF 2008)?

* Is nature central to children's experiences outdoors? Are there child gardens for children to dig, plant, tend and harvest and small natural spaces for children to create imaginary worlds? Are ecology and sustainability integral parts of your approach?

* Think about the learning potential of children experiencing fire outdoors. Are there safe ways you could include it in your garden or outdoor area?

7 The wider world of people and places

Teachers should regularly take their classes out of doors – not driving them like a flock of sheep or leading them as if they were a company of soldiers, but walking with them as a father with his sons or a brother with his brothers and making them more familiar with whatever Nature or the seasons offers.

(Froebel, in Lilley 1967: 146)

Froebel believed that the school or kindergarten should be closely connected to the surrounding community and landscapes. The local area, including the rivers, and streams, hills and forests, shops and trades offered rich opportunities for broadening children's experiences. There are examples of Froebel and children making dams in a local stream to investigate the flow of water. He also took children, each with a wheelbarrow, into the local streets to collect litter (Liebschner 1992).

Today, a Froebelian approach places great value on learning beyond the home or early years setting. Visits out to places of interest can energise, enthuse and inspire children and they can offer genuine first-hand experience which can extend their understanding of the world of people, places and things.

Local visits and walks

Young children's knowledge of their local environment and community can be limited because they are so often transported in cars or rushed from place to place in pushchairs, with little time or opportunity to share and talk about interesting things on the way. Yet local streets can offer intriguing and fascinating things for a toddler to explore. There are drains and grilles, fences with holes to push things through, gates to swing on, puddles to splash in and small creatures to investigate. Froebel suggested that for a toddler a walk is 'like a voyage of discovery and each new object is an America, a new world to explore' (Lilley 1967: 112).

A Froebelian approach includes regular visits out, sometimes just walks taken at a very slow pace, or walks to interesting places – for example, to a local market to buy ingredients for cooking, to a local post office to buy stamps and post letters, to a nearby printing press to collect offcuts of paper and card, or maybe to the garden of a bee-keeping parent to see the inside of a beehive.

Such visits can provide new experiences which link with the activities within the setting and also ensure that the setting is a visible part of the local community. I remember taking a group of children to the top of a nearby tower block which overlooked the nursery school so that they could experience height and perspective. They were amazed at how everything familiar in the nursery garden looked so small from such a height.

Visits are also arranged further afield, perhaps to a local farm, heliport, building site, museum or gallery. Such visits out are not just summertime 'treats' but are seen as an integral and regular part of the learning experience for children. For example, children in one London nursery school were involved in redesigning a part of their garden. This involved digging, moving soil and constructing a fountain. They went to visit fountains in nearby parks to help decide on the design and to think about how the fountains worked (Devereux and Bridges 2004).

The importance of such visits has been confirmed by contemporary research. For example, the Froebel Research Project (Athey 2007) identified how visits out to interesting places can enrich children's

School garden

learning. Children, parents and teachers went on weekly visits to such places as the zoo, airport and police stables, as well as local parks and woodland. Visits were carefully planned to enrich children's schemas – their patterns of behaviour which are repeated over and over again. For example children who were fascinated by things that spin round, a rotational schema, were taken to visit a local windmill or to experience a helter-skelter. The visits featured strongly in children's spontaneous drawings, paintings, models, talk and stories, showing that they were meaningful and significant. Research noted the vast increase in the amount of talk and that both children and parents barely paused for breath during projects. Clearly, rich experiences beyond the early years setting provide much to talk and think about.

Schemas

We sometimes run to catch up.

Forest Schools

The growing 'Forest School' movement offers regular experience outside the early years setting. The notion of Forest Schools resonates with Froebel's emphasis on the importance of children learning out-doors in contact with the natural world. Children as young as 2 or 3 spend up to a day a week in a local woodland area, accompanied by a Forest School leader and early years staff. There are no buildings, and little or no shelter, just maybe a canvas-covered area that provides some protection in very wet weather. Children play in the woods, climb trees, explore streams and ponds, wade through mud, slide down slopes, navigate ditches, build dens and fires and use real tools such as saws and knives. They experience the changing seasons and see how familiar space is transformed in subtle and sometimes dramatic ways. For example, the pond disappears in dry weather or becomes solid in icy weather.

growing + harvesting with our garden.

Children use all their senses to experience the natural world, such as the musty, damp smell of autumn, the sounds of the wind in the trees, the taste of freshly picked blackberries or the thrill of rolling down a grassy bank. They learn the importance of collaborating and working together – for example, in moving a very heavy log or using a rope to climb a steep, slippery bank. They learn how to assess and manage risk – for

Figure 7.1 Forest School affords opportunities for being adventurous and testing limits.

Figure 7.2 Demonstrating competence – 'I can do it.'

example, by using a stick to test out the depth of water in a stream or boggy area. Children are helped to overcome fears, such as getting lost or being out of sight of others, through simple hide and seek games.

Such experiences resonate strongly with a Froebelian approach. Froebel's ideas had a considerable influence on pedagogy and practice in Scandinavia where nature kindergartens are well-established parts of young children's experiences. The UK also has a tradition of Forest School-type experiences often pioneered by Froebelian teachers.

Recently there has been a growth of Forest Schools in urban areas (Milchem 2011). For example, children from a London nursery school and children's centre visit Wimbledon Common for a day a week, where they can climb trees, construct their own rope swings, paddle in small streams, and so on. The children in Figure 7.3 are using a rope to cross a ditch. They learn to collaborate together and to trust each other. They learn how to assess and manage risk – for example, by testing the tautness of the rope before putting their weight on it.

Milchem notes how strange and sometimes frightening the natural world can be for children who have not experienced it before. She

Figure 7.3 Collaborating together, using a rope to cross a deep ditch.

gives examples of how walking on bumpy, uneven surfaces or amongst thick fallen leaves can be distressing to some children whose previous experience of walking has been on flat, hard ground, manicured lawns or spongy safety surfaces (Milchem 2011).

While the Forest School environment is rich in potential, it is how it is used by children and adults that matters. The underpinning values are therefore crucial. A Froebelian approach views children as capable, curious, creative, adventurous and imaginative. Children's own interests and enquiries are built on and extended by adults. As Froebel pointed out:

> Children may spend all their time in the open air but may still observe nothing of the beauties of Nature and their influence on the human heart. The boy sees the significance . . . but if he does not find the same awareness in adults the seed of knowledge just beginning to germinate is crushed.
>
> (Froebel, in Lilley 1967: 146)

Conclusion

This chapter has looked at the importance of the wider world of people and places, whether urban streets or open, woodland spaces. Froebel believed that learning beyond the kindergarten was an important way of connecting children to the wider world and offered rich learning experiences, provided they are carefully thought about and considered by practitioners.

Bringing the Froebel approach to learning beyond the early years setting

- Are visits out a regular part of the home or group setting throughout the year?

- Are they closely linked to children's interests and concerns?

- Is the local area seen as a rich learning resource? Do children have opportunities for slow paced walks with adults, where they can discover and investigate fascinating things?

- Is there an area of local woodland or wild space that you could use on a regular basis as a Forest School? This might take time to develop but it's the commitment which is essential. Make contact with a local Forest School network for advice and training.

8 | Block play

> Simple playthings that allow children to feel and experience, to act and represent, and to think and recognise.
>
> (Froebel, cited in Brosterman 1997: 51)

Block play is an integral part of all Froebelian early years settings. The wooden modular 'unit' and 'hollow' blocks which are used today are larger versions of Froebel's 'gifts', boxed sets of blocks, divided in mathematically precise ways which Froebel designed for his kindergartens (see Chapter 5).

Froebel's blocks

Froebel intended the blocks to be used for children to represent:

- *forms of life*, using the blocks to create and represent things and events in the world around them
- *forms of beauty*, where the focus is on aesthetic aspects of pattern, order, symmetry and harmony
- *forms of knowledge*, exploring mathematical forms and scientific concepts such as shape, size, area, stability and balance.

Froebel saw the blocks as bringing together all areas of learning in a meaningful whole. They could promote imagination, creativity and symbolic thinking, as well as mathematical and scientific concepts. They helped develop understanding of pattern and design. Block play was also important for developing language, storytelling and singing, as adults and children created stories and songs around the block creations. The whole child is active – the doing, thinking, feeling and social self.

Children could choose how to use the blocks to represent objects and events that were significant in their own lives, as the following observation of children in Froebel's kindergarten illustrates:

> Little boxes of blocks are given to them, and they begin without delay to play eagerly. One child remembers how he has just had breakfast with his dear parents, and he quickly builds a table surrounded with chairs . . . Yonder a child shows us quite a different idea. He has seen a shepherd starting out in the early morning with his flock; and so he represents the shepherd prominently, with the sheep obediently following him. Thus each child follows his individual bent, according as the spirit moves him . . . Here is a boy who has built an anvil . . . There is a little girl who has built a town hall. Her father goes there every morning when she comes to kindergarten.
>
> (Middendorff 1848, in Owen 1906: 206–207)

Recently I observed children building 'a disco', 'Humpty Dumpty's wall' and 'shelves in a supermarket'. A group of children worked together to build an airport, complete with arrival and departure lounges, car parks, baggage scanners and circular baggage carousels. Blocks are timeless play materials which can cross generations and cultures.

The value of block play

Blocks are tools with which children can design, create, build, think, solve problems, imagine, communicate and reflect. Their simplicity allows for a myriad of different creative combinations, and children can use the blocks according to their experience and development. There is no one way of using them, just many possibilities.

Blocks as a symbolic language

Blocks are like a 'symbolic language' of shape, form and space. The unyielding nature of blocks compared with, say, the malleable nature of wet sand or clay offers both opportunities and limitations. With experience and support from others, children get to know the 'language' of blocks so that they can communicate their ideas with increasing fluency and complexity. Blocks help develop symbolic abstract thought because a structure can 'stand for' something else, the individual blocks taking on a new significance as part of the 'whole'.

Mathematical and scientific thinking

The modular nature of the blocks invites mathematical thinking as children experience geometric relationships – for example, wholes, halves, quarters and eighths. They begin to see mathematical relationships – for example, that two wedge-shape bricks can create a rectangular block and that four curved triangular pieces can create a complete circle. These concepts are experienced in meaningful ways long before children hear about 'fractions'.

In the course of their building, children confront significant engineering, scientific and design problems such as balance, gravity, weight, stability and symmetry and they begin to learn relationships of cause and effect.

Blocks and architecture

Blocks can give insights into the form and design of the built environment, including architectural features such as columns, arches, buttresses, gables and lintels. The renowned architect Frank Lloyd

Figure 8.1 Will this block fit in this space? Developing awareness of stability, balance, shape, size and position.

Wright claims that his childhood play with Froebel blocks shaped his passion for design. His mother was a Froebel-trained teacher and bought the blocks for him in 1876. He remembers the

> smooth, shapely maple blocks with which to build, the sense of which never after leaves the fingers: form becomes feeling . . . Here was something for invention to seize, and use to create. These gifts came into the gray house in drab old Weymouth, and made something live that had never lived before.
>
> (Lloyd Wright 1943: 13)

Many of Lloyd Wright's buildings show the formative influence of his early experiences of the blocks and some have even been recreated using the Froebel blocks.

Positive dispositions to learning

Block play requires perseverance, the willingness to solve problems, to cope with frustration, to reflect on experience, to modify ideas and to learn from mistakes. Successful block players develop sensitivity to others, a heightened awareness of their own and others' space and a willingness to negotiate and compromise. Block play is particularly valuable in developing these positive dispositions as children are motivated to want to continue the play.

Such is the richness of blocks that children can explore the realms of their imaginations but at the same time are confronted with real-world problems such as gravity and balance and the limitations of their own physical dexterity. As Froebel argued, the real and the pretend, the concrete and the abstract, the whole and the parts, freedom and constraint – are all inextricably connected in one play material.

Holistic learning

The children in Figure 8.2 have built a multi-storey car park. They collaborated together for over two hours. They overcame problems of

Figure 8.2 Sustained collaborative play, involving all areas of the curriculum.

balance and stability by realising that they had to support each platform with blocks of the same length. They created a helicopter pad on the top of the structure and then used paper straws and tape to create a ticket machine and an entrance/exit barrier.

Within this play we can see evidence of all areas of learning in the Early Years Foundation Stage (DCSF 2008):

- *Personal, Social and Emotional Development*: planning, negotiating, compromising; being aware of others in a small space; taking risks, for example balancing on a stepladder to reach the top; pride in achievement; perseverance, involvement, being autonomous and making choices and decisions.
- *Communication, Language and Literacy*: making tickets; using writing for a purpose; drawing and cutting out a large 'H' sign to place on the roof for the helicopter pad; noticing that H features as an initial letter in some children's names; using new words such as 'ramps', 'levels', 'helicopter pad' in a meaningful context. Interest in different meanings of similar-sounding words 'story' and 'storey'.
- *Problem-solving, Reasoning and Numeracy*: exploring height, pattern, shape and length, such as finding blocks the same length; understanding about levels; thinking about top and bottom – for example, the helicopter pad is on the top and the ticket machine is at the bottom of the building.
- *Knowledge and Understanding of the World*: understanding about how a car park works; solving problems in relation to stability; exploring gradients and ramps.
- *Physical Development*: care and precision in movements; strength in lifting and carrying heavy blocks; stretching and reaching; awareness of their own body in relation to space around them.
- *Creative Development*: designing, constructing, creating; being original; being imaginative; making connections with their own lives; thinking symbolically; awareness of balance and symmetry; using materials such as a paper straw and tape to make a 'barrier' that moves up and down.

Figure 8.3 Learning to share space and respect others' constructions.

The richness of blocks is that children experience so many areas of learning in one meaningful, collaborative, creative construction.

The Froebel Blockplay Research Project

The Froebel Blockplay Research Project (Gura 1992) noted that children used blocks in a variety of ways and that there are often patterns in how children use the blocks, such as:

- stacking vertically
- stacking horizontally
- bridging
- making slopes
- making enclosures

- edge bordering

- filling in

- making a central core with radials, or zigzag lines, or intersections or grids

- making symmetrical or asymmetrical structures

- putting blocks inside, outside, over, under, on, through, rotating

- transporting blocks from here to there and back.

(adapted from Gura 1992; Jenner 2010)

A Froebelian approach recognises the importance of children exploring their ideas through different media. For example, children who are fascinated by grid patterns may use blocks as well as other material such as paint, pens, clay or sand. Similarly, children who discover a spider's web and are fascinated by the core and radial structure may seek to create this in blocks as well as other media. By recognising these patterns in children's learning practitioners can extend children's thinking by enriching these 'schemas' with further provision (Louis *et al.* 2008).

Block play: the key role of the adult

Rich block play does not just occur. It develops when the adult acts as a powerful catalyst working hard to enable it.

(Bruce, in Gura 1992: 26)

Knowing about blocks

Froebel argued that educators should have a deep understanding of the learning potential of the blocks and the developmental aspects of block play as well as a practical understanding of the blocks themselves. Practitioners who play with the blocks on in-service training courses are often amazed to discover the richness of the materials which they had not fully appreciated before. They return to their settings with new insights into the possibilities of blocks.

Free choice

Froebelian educators value children's own play with blocks. They do not instruct, build structures for children to copy or impose adult-designed tasks. Instead, educators interact sensitively by carefully observing, tuning in to the child's intentions, actively listening, showing interest and respect for the children's constructions.

Free choice does not mean children doing just 'any old thing' with the blocks. Clear basic rules – for example, that blocks stay in the block area, that there is a storage place for every block and that constructions can only be knocked down with the builder's permission – can enhance all children's freedom to build.

Connections

Froebelian educators make connections with other areas of learning – for example, through finding relevant books, photos, stories, songs and rhymes or organising visits to see relevant features of the built environment linked with the children's structures. But, Froebel warned, these should be genuine connections, not forced, contrived links which have no meaning for children.

Links and connections can also be made with other areas of provision and recycled materials, pens, paper and tape are often combined with the symbolic representation. For example, the children in Figure 8.4 used wool to complete their representation of a spider's web. The children in Figure 8.5 fetched blankets and picnic baskets from the role play area to add to their block-built house.

Small world characters or natural materials such as pebbles, stones or shells can add to the design of the structures or to the storymaking. However, findings from the Froebel Block Play Project suggested that if these resources are provided too early, before children have gained

Figure 8.4 Using wool with the blocks to create a spider's web.

experience with the blocks themselves, they can inhibit the develop-ment of block play. Gura suggests that accessory materials are stored separately so that experienced players can choose to fetch them for a particular purpose but less experienced builders are not distracted by them (Gura 2002).

Space

Space needs to be flexible enough to allow block play to extend in unforeseen ways. A quiet location away from the main traffic flow ensures that play can continue without unnecessary interruption. There should be sufficient blocks to allow for large-scale, collaborative struc-tures as rich play does not develop if builders run out of blocks. Where possible, the provision of blocks outside allows large-scale collabora-tive constructions.

Figure 8.5 Using blocks with other materials for imaginative play.

Figure 8.6 Taking blocks outdoors. Here the children are
building a 'lorry for moving things'.

Displays of books, plans, photos of buildings, railways, bridges, temples, castles, patterns in nature, and so on can also be included in a block area. An archive of photos or sketches of previous constructions can be used as a memory bank, helping children to reflect back and think ahead, such as 'Do you remember when . . . ? Shall we build it the same, or different?'

Storage which shows the whole and the parts

Blocks should be freely available in open-access storage systems and not heaped together in a tub or basket. The storage system must help children to see the modular structure of the blocks as a whole system and begin to understand the mathematical relationships. This was very important to Froebel. As children select and return the blocks they can begin to see the geometrical relationships and how the parts relate to the whole.

Time

Block play requires extended periods of uninterrupted time. Children need plenty of practice to become confident builders. They do not invest great enthusiasm and energy in play with blocks if they know that it will soon be time to pack them away. As children become more experienced they often spend a whole session in the block area and even continue their ideas over a period of days. Children can be helped to record their constructions through photos or sketches. Notices requesting that the structure is left intact for another day can be written. For example, two 5-year-olds wrote this notice requesting that the building is left intact until the next day: 'PLES KEP AR BDNG NO NCNG DWN'.

Valuing block play

The more practitioners discuss and reflect on theory and practice, the more value and status they afford it. This heightened interest increases the enthusiasm and motivation of everyone – children, educators and parents.

One of the best ways that adults can raise the status of block play is by spending significant amounts of time in the block area. If adults avoid the block area or enter it only to sort out disputes, then children quickly learn that blocks are deemed less important than other areas of learning. Monitoring the gender balance of those using the area and ensuring that less experienced and confident children are able to access the space is also an essential part of the adult role.

Sensitive interaction

How adults support children's block play is central to a Froebelian approach. It is all too easy to dominate block play by hurrying children up, giving solutions to a problem before they have tried out ideas or taking over their play in unhelpful ways.

Sensitive interaction is about supporting and extending the play in ways which are appropriate to individuals or groups of children. This might involve:

- *Being a participative observer.* This signals active interest in what the children are doing and allows adults to observe closely at children's level. Being attentive and interested communicates respect for block play and encourages players who may be new to the area.
- *Listening.* This is more than just hearing what children say. It is about being open and curious and wanting to understand what children are trying to do. It is about trying to tune in to their ideas and thinking. It is also about resisting the urge to talk and interrupt the play.
- *Protecting children's block play.* Adults sometimes need to intervene to protect children's block-building space from others who are encroaching on it. However, helping children negotiate and find their own solutions to problems is important, and sometimes this involves 'watchful waiting' to see what strategies children them- selves use to solve disputes.

- *Being a play partner.* Joining in play can be an effective strategy, particularly for children who are new to blocks. Playing in parallel, for example, allows adults to observe children and play alongside them in a similar way.
- *Putting actions into words.* This can be helpful in fixing, through words, what a child is doing, enabling them to be more 'knowing' about their block building, for example, 'you've joined two short blocks to make one long block' or 'you've managed to bridge those two towers'. Introducing new words such as 'spanning' or 'buttressing' also draws attention to attributes of blocks and features of building.
- *Questioning.* Bombarding children with questions detracts from rich block play. However, occasional use of carefully chosen questions can help children to reflect on what they are doing, for example 'That's interesting – what made you think of that?' 'I wonder how you can make that more stable?' 'How do you think the Princess might get into your castle?'
- *Supporting and extending.* When observations of children are combined with sensitive intervention children's play can be extended, as the following example illustrates:

> The children are examining a spider's web outside. Ricci (4y.6m) is captivated and he draws it. He then decides to make one with blocks, using his drawing as a general guide. He has an excellent knowledge of blocks and his first steps involve negotiating for those he thinks he is going to need. His teacher records that she had to talk him through the construction of the concentric enclosures.
>
> In tackling the radials, he runs out of the longest blocks: 'I need more big blocks'. The adult offers an idea: 'Could you make that length by joining some of the shorter ones?'
>
> Given her knowledge of the child, his previous experience and her understanding of what he was trying to achieve . . . the adult was able to give the right degree of help at the right moment for him to succeed. She did it in a way that supported the play 'without dominating it' and avoided 'damaging the process of self-regulation'.
>
> (Froebel Blockplay Research Group, in Gura 1992: 127)

In summary

The Froebel Blockplay Research Project (Gura 1992) found that the participants' knowledge about the possibilities of blocks, research, observation, reflection and discussion led to increased enthusiasm and understanding, more informed interaction and further observation and research. Over the course of the project there was a profound increase in the complexity and richness of children's play in ways which were not envisaged at the start. We are only beginning to understand the potential of blocks as a tool for thinking, learning and creating, and there is still much work to be done.

Bringing the Froebel approach to block play

- Invest in sets of good-quality wooden blocks (see, for example, Community Playthings www.communityplaythings.com). Initial expenditure can be cost-effective because blocks are so long-lasting. Some local authorities consider blocks to be essential provision and have bought sets of blocks for all their private, voluntary and independent early years settings.

- Play with the blocks yourself. Find out the possibilities and limitations of blocks as a 'language'. Gura suggests starting by taking two quarter units and seeing how many *distinctly* different ways that you can find to put them together. The record, she believes, is 40 (Gura 1996: 38)!

- Think about time, space and adult involvement in your own setting.

- Observe what children are doing with the blocks. Make links with available research.

- Above all, get interested in and enthusiastic about blocks and their possibilities.

9 | Movement, song, rhythm and rhyme

Did you realise that the finger rhymes, action songs and ring games that you use with young children have their origins in Froebel's 'mother songs' and movement games? Froebel devised a series of some fifty finger rhymes, action songs and games for mothers and other family members to share with babies and young children at home. These were published as 'Mother Songs' although the original title referred to a 'Family Book'. Each song was carefully illustrated, with a series of pictures showing a story or series of events linked to the song, which mother and child could look at and talk about together. The illustrations also included sketches to show the appropriate finger and hand movements for the song.

Froebel argued that these were not just trivial amusements to occupy babies but provided key learning experiences. He placed infancy and mothers and babies learning together at home as of central importance in his educational approach. This was at a time when education began with sedentary instruction at school – and only men were viewed as educators.

In his writings Froebel explained the underpinning significance of the mother songs and finger rhymes. He emphasised the importance of:

- Close, intimate relationship between mother (or other family member) and child as they shared the finger rhymes. For example, the child should be sitting on the mother's lap and there should be a reciprocal, responsive relationship, where mothers pick up cues from babies as to what they are interested in.

- The powerful connections between movement, rhythm, rhyme and learning. Infants were not to be passively entertained but were to be actively involved through moving their limbs. The finger rhymes focused attention on hands and fingers in particular and helped to strengthen them. The action songs and ring games focused on developing whole-body movements and coordinating movement with others. Movement and mind, Froebel argued, are inextricably linked. For example, in one of the movement games called 'the cartwheel' a large outer ring and a smaller inner ring of children created the movement of the cartwheel, focusing attention on how the outer rim of the wheel moves faster than the inner rim. Children could experience this directly through movement.

- Developing awareness of symbols. The finger rhymes are important in developing children's awareness of symbolic representation. Fingers, movements or sounds can stand for something else. For example, in the rhyme 'Here is the beehive, where are the bees?' the position of the hands can represent the shape of the beehive or the movement of the bees, and the bzzzz sound can represent the sound of the bees. Gaining fluency in the use of symbols is vital for communicating through a range of symbolic languages such as music, dance, drawing and painting, as well as spoken and written languages.

- Meaningful connections between the songs and rhymes and the child's own life. The mother can help to make links with the child's experience and the wider world. For example, the illustrations for the song 'Pat-a-cake' showed links between the corn growing in the field, the miller, the flour, the baker and the eventual cake, illustrating how all of these are connected.

- Respect for others. The content of the songs, Froebel argued, can foster abstract ideas of goodness, generosity, respect for others and connectedness. For example, a song about the charcoal burner emphasised respect for the work of all people regardless of their appearance or status in society. The illustrations showed how the baby was connected to the charcoal burner as he provided the wood for the fire which melted the iron which formed the metal which made the spoon which was used for the baby's food. Such abstract ideas were clearly way beyond infants' understanding but Froebel argued that the germ of the seed was planted which, if nurtured, could develop and ripen over time.

Froebel's ideas were way ahead of his time. The idea that mothers were key educators of their children, and that pictures, songs and rhymes enjoyed in a warm, loving relationship on mothers' laps were important educational tools for babies and small children must have been considered revolutionary in the culture and context in which Froebel lived. However Froebel's mother songs have been criticised for their rather obscure symbolic meanings and the poor quality of the verses, and Froebel himself acknowledged that he was no poet. However, it was the underpinning principles, rather than the specific songs, which Froebel considered important and which continue to have significance today (see, for example, Baker 2012).

Contemporary research

Research today confirms the immense significance and foresight of Froebel's ideas. For example, Colwyn Trevarthen (1995) identified the importance of the universal shared exchanges between baby and parent or carer for developing communication and what he refers to as 'proto-conversations'. He illustrates the dance-like way that attuned mothers and babies interact together, each responding to the other in often perfect synchrony and harmony. We also know about the importance of talking with babies long before they can understand the meaning of words, interpreting their gestures and vocalisations as though they have meaning (Wells 1986).

Research on the development of language and literacy (for example Whitehead 2007) shows the importance of sharing books with babies and young children in warm, intimate settings, turning the pages, scanning the pictures for meaning, focusing closely on small details in the illustrations and enjoying the repetition of familiar phrases and sounds. Relating the pictures and events in the story to the child's own life ensures that there is a meaningful connection and helps develop new vocabulary in ways that make sense.

Young children's awareness of rhyme is a powerful predictor of later success in reading. As research by Goswami has shown, children who have good rhyming skills are much better at making analogies and become better readers than children who have poor rhyming skills (cited in Whitehead 2007). Many traditional songs and contemporary jingles draw attention to features of language. For example, the clapping game 'A sailor went to sea, sea, sea to see what he could see, see, see' focuses attention on alliteration and double meanings. Such rhymes are important ways that children begin to understand that a spoken word is a symbol which can stand for more than one thing.

The rhymes and rhythms of many of the traditional finger and nursery rhymes, accompanied by actions of hand clapping, finger tapping, body swaying, or foot stamping, develop an awareness of 'beat' and love for the musicality of language which is crucial for the enjoyment of poetry, literature, music and drama.

Evidence from neuroscience shows the importance of movement, music and dance in building the circuitry of the brain. Finger rhymes and movement games help motor development, and stimulate the senses of balance and space, all of which are needed for such things as reading, writing, riding a bike, and so on (Goddard-Blyth 2011).

Sharing familiar rhymes creates gurgles of laughter and delight as babies anticipate what is coming next – for example, the tickling in the finger rhyme 'Round and round the garden' or the ' down in the ditch' in the bouncing rhyme 'This is the way the ladies ride'. In such intimate and secure contexts babies enjoy the thrill of being thrown in the air or falling backwards and experience the enjoyable sensation of being on the edge of feeling safe and unsafe. They experience small amounts of risk and uncertainty in safe and pleasurable ways (Tovey 2012).

Jenny Spratt, former Head of Early Years and Childcare Services in Peterborough, researched finger rhymes as part of her studies for a Froebel Diploma at Roehampton University, London. She found that it was helpful to start first with rhymes which use the whole hand and all ten fingers, then to move to rhymes which focus attention on certain

Figure 9.1 Finger rhymes and clapping games integrate movement, language, rhythm and rhyme, and link with the wider world.

fingers and then to rhymes where the fingers represent things symbolically. Her research emphasised the importance of adults and children tracking the movement of their fingers and of sharing rhymes in small groups, so that adults can really see how children move their fingers with the rhymes (Bruce and Spratt 2011).

Action rhymes, movement and ring games

Action songs such as 'Wind the bobbin up' or 'Roly poly' involve the coordination of movement, language, rhythm and vision. It can be very challenging for young children to coordinate their upper body movements with the sounds of the rhymes – for example, in making their arms move in a circular motion, gradually increasing height to the words 'roly, poly, up up up'. The rhythm, words and repetition support the actions, and help fix the words and actions in the memory. Standing up action songs such as 'If you're happy and you know it clap your

Figure 9.2 Playing with rhythm and rhyme,
singing 'Izzy Wizzy, let's get busy'.

hands' involve upper and lower parts of the body and sometimes the coordination of, say, clapping and stamping. Bruce and Spratt (2011) point out that it is helpful for children to have lots of practice with these before moving on to ring games such as 'The Hokey Cokey', which require more complex coordination of movements with others.

As well as the strong links with literacy, many finger rhymes, action songs and ring games can develop language associated with simple counting – for example, 'One, two, three four five, once I caught a fish alive', or with counting and taking away – for example, 'Five little monkeys, jumping on the bed' or 'Five currant buns'. Other songs focus on spatial concepts, such as up, down, round, in, out, under, far away, and so on. 'The Hokey Cokey', for example, focuses attention on left, right, in, out and turning around, and 'Five little ducks' focuses on 'over the hill and far away'. All of these spatial concepts are linked with movements. Mathematical concepts can therefore be emphasised in a meaningful context.

Singing, both planned and spontaneous

Singing, as Froebel emphasised, creates joyfulness, group cohesion and a sense of community. It can be an important way of reinforcing everyday events and routines, reflecting on things that have happened and calming distressed or anxious children. Regular songs connected with significant routines and times of the day, such as greeting and parting songs ('Tick, tock, time to go') are important ways of creating a regular rhythm to the day. A singing voice attracts children's attention far more easily than a normal voice and it is often easier to get things done accompanied by a song – for example, 'This is the way we pick up the blocks, pick up the blocks, pick up the blocks . . .'

The repetitive rhythm and beat of songs means that it is easy to adapt well-known songs for a new purpose. For example, the familiar tune of 'Here we go round the mulberry bush' can be very useful to accompany actions with words in almost any context, such as when exploring the clay.

This is the way we bang the clay, bang the clay, bang the clay,
This is the way we bang the clay,
Bang, bang, bang.
This is the way we poke the clay . . .
This is the way we roll the clay . . .
This is the way we squeeze the clay . . .
This is the way we flatten the clay . . .
This is the way we smooth the clay . . .

A Froebelian approach places great emphasis on the power of movement, song and rhyme, and outbreaks of spontaneous singing – whether initiated by adults or by children – are a frequent occurrence. Songs and rhymes can become a taken-for-granted feature in many early years settings. However, by focusing more closely on their underpinning significance in relation to children's development, educators can observe children in more informed ways and can adjust their interactions and provision for individual children much more successfully (Ouvry 2012).

Conclusion

This chapter has looked at why movement, song, rhythm and rhyme are so fundamental to children's learning and to a Froebelian approach. It has made strong links with contemporary understandings of the importance of such songs and rhymes in developing communication, language and literacy.

Bringing the Froebel approach to movement, song, rhythm and rhyme

These are a few ways that you can develop a Froebelian approach in your own practice:

- Providing a wide range of finger rhymes, action songs and nursery rhymes for individuals, groups, indoors, outdoors and at all times of the day, not just in group sessions, making repeated use of well-loved favourites.

- Adapting familiar songs and rhymes to use in many different contexts in the nursery – for, say, splashing in the water, jumping in the mud, banging the clay, tidying up, washing hands, and so on.

- Playing with very familiar rhymes, making up new versions or deliberately turning them around and making nonsense, for example 'Hickory dickory dare, Runa flew up in the air'. Encouraging children to play with language and make up new verses for familiar rhymes.

- Making sets of 'poetry cards' which are rhymes written on a large card in the shape of the theme of the rhyme. For example 'Jelly on a plate' could be written on a large, jelly-mould-shaped piece of card so that children can recognise the rhyme and then follow the words (Figure 9.3). Note that the words 'wibble' and 'wobble' have been written in wobbly print, helping to emphasise their meaning.)

- Using props to help children with English as an additional language to understand the meaning of the rhyme. This might include

Figure 9.3 Poetry cards offer an important way into understanding print and linking letters, words and sounds in a meaningful way.

puppets, or cardboard cut-outs of a rabbit and a fly for the rhyme 'Little Peter Rabbit has a fly on his nose', or a clock and a mouse for 'Hickory, dickory dock' or props for 'Five little ducks went swimming one day'.

- Linking songs and rhymes to interesting events. For example, linking 'Insy Winsy Spider' after watching a spider, or 'Little Arabella Miller' after finding a caterpillar.

- Extending songs and rhymes into all areas of the early years setting. For example, building a Humpty Dumpty wall with bricks and cement, making pease pudding, or constructing a dingle dangle scarecrow with a flippy floppy hat for the vegetable garden. This enables lots of repetition and helps the meaning of the rhyme to come alive.

- Looking deeper into *why* the songs and rhymes are significant in all areas of children's development and learning is important, so that educators understand the underpinning rationale.

- Working in partnership with parents to share rhymes from a range of cultural traditions is an important way of ensuring continuity between home and nursery. It is fascinating to hear how similar intonations and rhyming words cross cultures. Making a simple book of well-loved rhymes, illustrated by children, together with a CD recording, allows parents to enjoy sharing the songs and rhymes with their children at home.

- Ensuring that enjoyment and delight are at the centre of all the songs and rhymes. They should not be mere time fillers at the end of the session, or didactic exercises used to make a teaching point out of context. The learning comes from how the educator uses the songs and rhymes, ensuring they are appropriate to children's developing abilities, are connected to the everyday interests and events in the setting and have enjoyment and close relationships at their centre.

10 | Adult roles and relationships

A key element of the Froebelian approach is the role of the educator. It is the adult who shapes the ethos and expectations of the setting, fosters the relationships, and enables children's learning. Froebel emphasised the complexity of the adult role:

> The true educator and teacher has to be at every moment and in every demand two-sided. He must give and take, unite and divide, order and follow; he must be active and passive, decisive and permissive, firm and flexible.
>
> (Froebel, in Lilley 1967: 55)

The crucial dimension is the sensitivity of the adult, the ability to adjust his or her interactions to the child and the context, and the understanding to make informed judgements. Clearly this is a demanding task which is why Froebel argued for specialist well-trained kindergarten teachers who are able to reflect on and develop their own practice.

This chapter looks at just some of the key roles of the adult, including:

- observing, supporting and extending play and learning
- encouraging children's curiosity and questions
- helping children reflect, and extending their thinking
- talking and discussing

- supporting children to solve their own problems

- helping children develop self-discipline

- working in partnership with parents.

Observing, supporting and extending play and learning

Observation of children underpins the Froebel approach. Observation allows the adult to tune in to the child, interact in a way which is meaningful and sensitive, and use the observations to support the child's learning and to inform interaction and subsequent planning. Observations are also important for the adult to think about, reflect on and perhaps question aspects of policy and practice.

Observation means much more than just watching. It means listening carefully, being open and wanting to know more. It means really taking note of what the child is interested in, thinking and feeling, and striving to understand what the child means or is trying to do. Observation-led planning is enshrined in the Early Years Foundation Stage. 'All planning starts with observing children in order to understand and consider their current interests, development and learning' (DCSF 2008).

Froebel emphasised the importance of observation, and his writings include many detailed observations of babies and young children. He argued that it is not enough just to give material resources, rather we need to identify the underpinning processes of children's learning and development in order to take learning forward. Isolated observations are not sufficient. To be meaningful, they need to be considered in the context of the whole child.

He was possibly the first educator to argue for individual child records, where 'the most important facts about each separate child could be recorded' (Froebel, in Lilley 1967). Today, such records or profiles are considered central to effective practice.

Tina Bruce argues that the essence of the adult role in a Froebelian setting is for the adult to 'observe, support and extend' (Bruce 1997: 97). She goes on to explain what this might involve:

Observation means using theory and research to inform both on the spot and reflective understanding about play between adults and children. **Supporting** begins where the child is and what the child can do. **Extending** might be to give help with physical materials, create space, give time, dialogue and converse about the play idea, or help with access strategies for the child to enter into play with other children. Extending also involves sensitivity and adding appropriately stimulating material provision and the encouragement of the child's autonomous learning.

(Bruce 1997: 97)

Encouraging children's curiosity and questions

Children are intensely curious about the world of people and things around them. Their curiosity can be seen in the explorations of the youngest children but, increasingly, children use questions to reveal their puzzlement and surprise about features of the world around them. For example:

* How do worms breathe under there? Why don't they sufferate?

* How do snails eat lettuce when they haven't any teeth?

* Why do men hoover the grass? [A 3-year-old watching gardeners mow the grass.]

* Why does it [a duckling] drink water like that, with its neck like that? Why doesn't it drink like a cat? I know – 'cos it hasn't got a tongue?

Such questions need more than just a stimulating environment to thrive. They require adults who invite such questions by being open and available, who treat a child's ideas as worthy of respect and who are willing to respond in a way that engages the child in further enquiry. Children's questions do not thrive in environments where adults ask all the questions.

Questions are an important way that children and adults can engage in extended conversation or 'sustained shared thinking'. The Froebel

Figure 10.1 Shared attention, focusing on the
peppers on the capsicum plant.

Research Fellowship Project, 'The Voice of the Child: Ownership and Autonomy in Early Learning', which focused on children's creative thinking, found that child-initiated activities were especially supportive of children's involvement in creative thinking, with outdoors being particularly valuable (Fumoto *et al.* 2012).

The role of the adult as a 'conversational partner' is also crucial in supporting and extending children's enquiry, as the following example illustrates:

Oliver (3 years 10 months) found a conker in the nursery pond, which he brought to show an adult.

Oliver:	It's darker, isn't it?
Adult:	Mmm, it's turned black.
Oliver:	Why's it's turned black?
Adult:	I'm not sure. Maybe because it's been in the water a long time.
Oliver:	Yes, 'cos conkers are brown, but this is black. I'm going to dry it on a tissue (*moves indoors*).

> Oliver: It's still dark 'cos, 'cos if you put a brown conker in white water, it goes black doesn't it, 'cos brown and white make black, don't they?
>
> Adult: That's interesting. We could try that tomorrow with some paint – try mixing it up to see. I think the conker is dark because it soaked up lots of water – look, like the tissue, where it's soaked up water it's gone darker.
>
> Oliver: (playing with tissue and conker in sink) If you put soap on and put all water on, it will go darker.

Here Oliver initiates a conversation expressing surprise that a conker which he knew to be brown was now black, showing the powerful curiosity and desire to make sense of a 3-year-old's mind. Adult and child negotiate meanings together which help shape the direction of his enquiry. The conversational structure clearly enhances the enquiry. Child initiates – adult responds and enlarges – child builds on answer and asks question – adult answers by reflecting on what is already known – child builds on answer and constructs his own explanation – and so on. The role of the adult in supporting and extending children's curiosity and creating a favourable environment for such enquiry is a significant part of the Froebel approach.

Helping children reflect, and extending their thinking

> The first and weightiest point of education is to lead children early to reflect.
>
> (Froebel, cited in Herford 1916: 45)

Froebel argued that self-activity on its own was not enough. Children should become aware of their own learning so that they 'know' some-thing in a deeper, more self-reflective way. Today we might call this 'metacognition', 'thinking about your own thinking' or self-regulation.

Research suggests that if adults use a range of thinking words such as 'think', 'know', 'remember', 'expect', 'guess', 'consider', 'reconsider',

Figure 10.2 An adult supporting and extending play. She poses a question:
'I wonder what will happen if I let it go?' They discuss ways
of making the structure more stable.

'wonder', 'imagine', 'decide' in everyday conversation, then children themselves come to think and talk like this (Astington 1994).

Open-ended questions, such as 'I wonder why that happened, I wonder what would happen if . . .', help children to reflect and invite speculation and consideration. They pose a question but do not demand a response. It is curiosity which is the key. Children need to believe that adults are interested in their ideas and that a question is a genuine attempt to understand their ideas or clarify their thinking. Well-timed questions which are used sparingly and are attuned to the child's focus of interest can take children's learning forward. This can be seen in the following exchange, when an adult probed children's under-standing of a pulley for transporting sand across the outdoor play area. The adult approached the issue in an indirect way:

Adult: I wonder what that rope at the top is for?
Benedict: Mmm, well, you see, when this one gets broken, then we could use that one instead.
Adult: I see. So where does the rope go when you do all that pulling?
Benedict: It goes in the wall.
Lauren: It stretches longer when you pull it.

It seemed that children conceived the pulley as an extendable single rope rather than a circular system. The higher rope was seemingly disconnected from the lower rope. Without saying anything, the adult tied another bucket on to the higher rope. The children's thinking was immediately challenged as they could see that there was a connection between both ropes as they moved in synchrony, one bucket moving forwards and the other bucket moving backwards. Later Benedict exclaimed, 'Look, when I pull [the rope] the bucket goes this way and the other bucket goes that way!'

This clearly illustrates the essence of the adult role as one of observing carefully, supporting, in this case posing a well-timed question, and extending, by adjusting the resources in a way that would challenge their thinking and help children see a cause-and-effect relationship.

Figure 10.3 Listening to children's ideas and
helping them solve their own problems.

Talking and discussing

Listening to children's ideas and theories offers remarkable insights into
their thinking and understanding. Sometimes group discussions, where
the context makes sense to children, allow ideas to be bounced around,
so children increasingly listen to and comment on others' ideas.

The following discussion was based on the Aesop fable about a bird
that could not drink from a narrow-topped container because his beak
was unable to reach the water. The problem was presented to a group
of 4-year-olds using simple props. Ideas flowed immediately:

Oliver: He can tip the pot over and then drink the water when it
spills.

Adult: That's a good idea isn't it? But then all the water would
be spilt and he wouldn't have any for tomorrow.

Oliver: Then just tip it a little bit then.

Charles: Oh, oh can I tell you something? When you make a hole then it come out whoosh and he could drink. He could peck a hole there (*points to the bottom of the pot*) and it would come out – whoosh.

Grace: Or he could just go to his house to the tap.

Vanessa: I know, he could get a pumper thing.

Tullulah: He could get a bowl a little bit round and have a drink.

Adult: Do you mean pour it into a bowl?

Tullulah: Yes – a round bowl.

Matthew: His neck can get really long again and then his neck can get a drink of water then.

Adult: How can his neck get longer?

Matthew: He could eat all his food.

Davinia: No, it'll be too long a wait. He could drink a magic drink and say 'Grow neck' and it will be magicked longer.

Emily: If we could get a knife and cut the top off and then he could reach it.

The variety of solutions reveals a wide range of different understandings as well as ways of thinking about the problem. The context is meaningful and makes sense and provides a shared frame of reference for ideas to be explored. There is no right answer, and this provides scope for a rich variety of possibilities, all of which are valid but are also open to doubt. Interestingly 'growing a long neck by eating food' is rejected as 'too long a wait'. To Davinia, a magic answer fits more easily.

When some of these children were later presented with a real problem – how can the ducklings drink from a half-filled jar of water, the answer was unanimous – pour it out into a lower, smaller or flatter pot. Reality can often be quite mundane, but story and play allow 'possibility' ideas to flow in more creative ways.

Supporting children to solve their own problems

The instinct for adults to step in and solve problems for children is strong, but a problem can be a rich source of learning, as the following example from Lynn McNair, a Froebelian educator and head of Cowgate Under 5s Centre, Edinburgh, illustrates:

> A group of children are throwing a bean bag in the garden when it becomes stuck on the window ledge of my office. 'Oh no' exclaims a voice, 'Lynn, help us'. I wander over and survey the situation. 'I wonder what we can do?' I muse. The children all talk at once, swapping ideas and suggestions. They begin to collect the bread crates, forming a pile and attempting to climb them. With each crate, a different child climbs atop it, trying to reach the window ledge. I watch quietly, ready to assist if needed, but not interfering with their scheme. They determine that the crates are just not high enough.
>
> 'We need something big!' exclaims Joe, 'really big!' Together he and I find a bamboo pole in the cupboard. He attempts to climb atop the crates, pole in hand, quickly determines the difficulty, so asks a friend to hold it. Once the summit is reached, he asks for the pole, and with a little waving about, dislodges the bean bag and sends it falling to the ground. His friends cheer as he climbs down, flushed with his success. I could have helped them by getting the bean bag down, but where's the learning in that?
>
> (Cowgate Under 5s Centre, http://www.cowgateunder5s.co.uk)

This example illustrates the importance of informed decisions as to when to step in and when to hold back. This involves knowing the children well, trusting children to see their ideas through, despite the element of risk, and empowering children to see themselves as competent problem solvers. As Claxton has argued:

> Rushing in and rescuing children prematurely deprives them of the opportunity to flex their learning muscles and also to get used to the emotions which accompany such difficulties – frustration . . . apprehension and so on.
>
> (Claxton 1999: 265)

Helping children develop self-discipline

Froebel argued that adults should help children develop self-discipline. He believed that children are inherently good and want to please, and that behind a misdemeanour there is often a good intention which adults need to identify and build on. Poor behaviour can reflect events in the child's life which adults need to recognise and work with. Froebel also argued that children should be quietly helped to see the impact of their own behaviour.

A Froebelian approach always starts where the child is, not where the adult thinks they should be. The adult observes carefully, develops children's interests and fascinations, and gently develops the positive aspects of a child's behaviour while also building a close and consistent relationship. Misdemeanours are talked through, so that the child can begin to see the impact of their actions on others. There are no external reward systems such as star charts, stickers or prizes in a Froebelian approach. Rather, children's own efforts and achievements and their pleasure in others' response to small acts of kindness are considered more powerful incentives than external rewards.

Working in partnership with parents

Froebel believed that educators should work closely with parents so that there was a close connection between kindergarten and home. A child should feel a sense of harmony and continuity between kinder-garten and home, not a sharp division. Educators should find the common threads that can bind a community together, the unity in diversity.

Athey's research confirmed how powerful this partnership can be when professionals and parents really work together and share their own insights and knowledge of individual children. A key finding of the Froebel Early Education Research Project was that all the adults involved, parents and professionals, listened with ever-increasing interest to what the children were saying and doing as they shared examples of their children's schemas.

The following example is just one of many documenting how parents and educators worked together:

> Shanaz [3 years 11 months] described a picture she had drawn as 'big, big flowers growing up in a big, big house and the girl going down that' (pointing to a drawing of a ladder). Shanaz's mother, who spoke very little English, understood Shanaz's powerful 'grid' schema. Together they made a book at home that consisted of cut out pictures and drawings of all the grid-like objects in the home.
>
> (Athey 1990: 64)

Athey found that at the beginning of the project there was a wide gulf between parents and professionals because of a lack of shared understanding. However, this disappeared as they searched for shared areas of agreement as to how to help individual children. Athey concluded that:

> Nothing gets under the parent's skin more quickly and more permanently than the illumination of his or her own child's behaviour. The effect of participation can be profound.
>
> (Athey 1990: 66)

Ways to share information with parents can be found when there is a genuine desire and commitment to do so. As a headteacher of a nursery school, I learnt very quickly that sending out letters inviting parents to a meeting and then complaining when few turned up was not the way to approach a positive partnership. Being sensitive to parents' different starting points, finding common points of interest, listening to parents, creating a shared sense of excitement about children's learning was much more appropriate. Video clips of children's learning can be particularly successful in helping to gain parents' as well as children's perspectives (Greenfield 2012).

Bringing the Froebel approach to adult roles and relationships

- Does observation really shape your interaction with children and inform your planning? How can you use your observations to support and extend children's learning?

- Try taping or filming yourself. How responsive is your interaction with children? Do you really listen and tune in to what they are doing and trying to communicate or do you dominate the talk and ask lots of questions?

- How imaginative and creative are children in their thinking? Are there opportunities for children to pursue their curiosity, to engage in open-ended exploration, speculation and 'possibility thinking'? Are their ideas treated with interest and respect?

- Try allowing children more time to solve their own problems. You might be surprised at the solutions they come up with!

Conclusion

This chapter has focused on the complex role of the adult, the central importance of informed observation of children and the need to tune in to children's ideas and emotions. Underpinning the adult role is a respect for children, a willingness to engage with children's ideas and preoccupations and a desire to support and extend their learning in meaningful and worthwhile ways. This requires knowledge of children, the contexts of their lives, the processes of their learning and the ability to reflect thoughtfully and critically on one's own practice. The ideas of Froebel provide a framework for such reflection, alongside contemporary understandings. By returning to and examining Froebel's ideas and those of other pioneers, we can enrich and sharpen our own.

Final words

This book has examined some key principles underpinning a Froebelian approach and what they might look like in practice. It has emphasised that a Froebelian approach is not a method and there is no standard 'one size fits all' approach. Rather, Froebelian settings may look very different in different contexts but will share the same guiding principles and a deep respect for young children as powerful learners and communicators. A Froebelian approach is not static but is continually evolving as ideas are reflected on and adapted for changing times and uncertain futures.

The last words belong to Froebel:

> Let us then secure for our children that which we lack ourselves. Let us transfuse from their lives into ours that vital creative energy of child life which we have lost. Let us learn from our children. Let us attend to the knowledge which their lives gently urge upon us and listen to the quiet demands of their hearts. Let us live for our children; then will their lives bring us joy and peace and we shall ourselves begin to grow into wisdom.
>
> (Froebel 1886: 92)

Appendix 1:
Key principles
underpinning a
Froebelian approach

Respect

- Early childhood is important in its own right and not merely a preparation for later learning. Learning begins at birth and continues throughout life.

- Children should be seen as 'essential members of humanity' and respected as 'living, loving and perceptive' people. Each child should be respected for 'who he is, what he has and what he will become' (Froebel, in Lilley 1967: 95).

- We should recognise the inherent good in children, building on what they can do rather than focusing on the negative. Children should be encouraged towards self-discipline.

Community

- Inclusion, diversity, belonging, close partnership with parents, families and community are key features of a harmonious learning community.

- The social and emotional wellbeing of a child is of central importance to their development and learning. Children should feel respected, thought about and understood and have a sense of belonging within a cohesive learning community.

Connectedness

- All aspects of a child's learning are interrelated and should be experienced as a meaningful whole.
- Making connections between what is new and what is known is a powerful aspect of learning.
- Seeing connections between opposites can be an important aspect of learning.
- The early years setting should be closely connected with the life of home, family, culture and local community.

Learning and development

- Learning should be joyous, meaningful and relevant. It should inspire further learning or it is nothing.
- Young children are active learners and learn best through first-hand experience, play, representation, talk and reflection.
- Relationships with others, both adults and children, are key to the learning process.
- Free movement, free choice and self-activity are important, but within a framework of guidance in which the role of the adult is crucial.

Creativity

- Education should cultivate children's essential creativity.
- Creativity and imagination are of central importance to children's learning. They are not optional extras or peripheral.
- Creativity enables children to make connections between their inner world of feelings and ideas and their outer world of things and experiences, and to reflect on them both.

Environment

- Direct, everyday experience of the natural world outdoors is essential so that children can learn to appreciate its wonders and begin to understand the ecological interrelationship between all living things.

- The environment, indoors and outdoors, should be emotionally safe and intellectually challenging, promoting friendships, curiosity, enquiry, creativity and a spirit of adventure.

- Simple, but carefully thought-about, open-ended resources, such as wooden blocks, have rich, multifaceted learning potential.

Well-qualified early years professionals

- Young children are entitled to knowledgeable and well-qualified professionals who are deeply informed about and attuned to the distinctive nature of young children's learning and development.

- Close observation of children's spontaneous play and learning informs and guides future planning as well as the adults' own understanding.

- Relationships with children should be close, trusting, responsive, interactive and intellectually engaging.

Appendix 2: Further information about Froebel and a Froebelian approach

The Froebel Trust

The Froebel Trust is a charity which promotes Froebelian principles and practice through research, conferences, courses and pioneering educational projects.

www.froebeltrust.org.uk

Froebel Archive for Childhood Studies, University of Roehampton, London

The Froebel Archive for Childhood Studies is a collection of books, archives, photographs, objects and multimedia materials related to Friedrich Froebel's legacy. It also includes a selection of digitized archive texts to read or download.

http://www.roehampton.ac.uk/Courses/Froebel-Archive-for-Childhood-Studies

International Froebel Society

The International Froebel Society provides an international forum for the development of the principles of educational theory and practice associated with Friedrich Froebel. The website includes information about conferences and has useful links to other websites related to Froebel.

http://www.intfroebelsoc.org

The Froebel Web

The Froebel Web is an online forum offering information about Froebel and resources, a useful timeline, bibliography and access to relevant texts.

www.froebelweb.org.uk

Courses on Froebelian principles and practice today

Details of Froebel Certificate Courses can be obtained from the School of Education, Froebel College, University of Roehampton, London.

www.roehampton.ac.uk

Resources and supporting materials

Community Playthings, based in Robertsbridge, Sussex, UK, sells wooden units and hollow blocks and many other resources. The website includes access to useful articles, practical guidance and downloadable publications.

http://www.communityplaythings.co.uk

Bibliography

Astington, J. (1994) *The Child's Discovery of the Mind.* London: Fontana.

Athey, C. (1990) *Extending Thought in Young Children: A Parent–Teacher Partnership.* London: Paul Chapman.

Athey, C. (2007) *Extending Thought in Young Children: A Parent–Teacher Partnership* (2nd edition). London: Paul Chapman.

Baker, M. (2012) Family songs in the Froebelian tradition. In Bruce, T., *Early Childhood Practice: Froebel Today.* London: Sage.

Brehony, K. (2006) Back to nature. *Nursery World,* August.

Brosterman, N. (1997) *Inventing Kindergarten.* New York: Abrams.

Brown, S. (2009) *Play: How it Shapes the Brain, Opens the Imagination and Invigorates the Soul.* New York: Penguin.

Bruce, T. (1997) Adults and children developing play together. *European Early Childhood Education Research Journal,* 5(1), 89–99.

Bruce, T. (2004) *Developing Learning in Early Childhood.* London: Paul Chapman.

Bruce, T. (2011a) Froebel today. In Miller, L. and Pound, L., *Theories and Approaches to Learning in the Early Years.* London: Sage.

Bruce, T. (2011b) *Early Childhood Education* (4th edition). London: Hodder.

Bruce, T. (2011c) All about . . . Friedrich Froebel. *Nursery World,* 7 April, 15–19.

Bruce, T. (ed.) (2012) *Early Childhood Practice: Froebel Today.* London: Sage.

Bruce, T. and Spratt, J. (2011) *Essentials of Literacy from 0–7* (2nd edition). London: Sage.

Bruce, T., McNair, L. and Siencyn, S. (2008) *I Made a Unicorn! Open Ended Play with Blocks and Simple Materials*. Robertsbridge: Community Playthings.

Claxton, G. (1999) *Wise Up: The Challenge of Life Long Learning*. London: Bloomsbury.

Department for Children, Schools and Families (DCSF) (2008) *Early Years Foundation Stage*. Nottingham: DCSF.

Department for Education (DfE) (2012) *Statutory Requirements for the Early Years Foundation Stage*. Runcorn: Cheshire DfE.

Devereux, J. and Bridges, A. (2004). Knowledge and understanding of the world developed through a garden project. In Miller, L. and Devereux, J., *Supporting Children's Learning in the Early Years*. London: David Fulton.

Elfer, P., Goldschmied, E. and Selleck, D. (2012) *Key Persons in the Early Years: Building Relationships for Quality Provision in Early Years Settings and Primary Schools*. London: Routledge.

Fjortoft, I. (2004) Landscapes as playscape: The effects of natural environments on children's play and motor development. *Children, Youth and Environments*, 14(2), 21–44.

Froebel, F. (1886) *Autobiography of Friedrich Froebel* (translated by Michaelis, E. and Moore, H.K.). London: Swan Sonnenschein.

Fumoto, H., Robson, S., Greenfield, S. and Hargreaves, D. (2012) *Young Children's Creative Thinking*. London: Sage.

Goddard-Blyth, S. (2011) *The Genius of Natural Childhood*. Stroud: Hawthorn.

Goldschmied, E. and Jackson, S. (1994) *People under Three: Young Children in Day Care*. London: Routledge.

Goldschmied, E. and Jackson, S. (2003) *People under Three: Young Children in Day Care* (2nd edition). London: Routledge.

Greenfield, S. (2012) Parents' experiences of supporting young children's creative thinking. In Fumoto, H. *et al.*, *Young Children's Creative Thinking*. London: Sage.

Greenland, P. (2006) Physical development. In Bruce, T. (ed.) *Early Childhood: A Guide for Students*. London: Sage.

Gura, P. (ed.) (1992) *Exploring Learning: Young Children and Blockplay*. London: Paul Chapman.

Gura, P. (1996) *Resources for Early Learning: Children, Adults and Stuff.* London: Hodder & Stoughton.

Gura, P. (ed.) (2002) *Exploring Learning: Young Children and Blockplay* (2nd edition). London: Paul Chapman.

Gussin Paley, V. (2010) *The Boy on the Beach: Building Community through Play.* London: University of Chicago Press.

Herford, W. (1916). *The Student's Froebel.* London: Pitman & Sons.

Jenner, F. (2010) *Block Play: A Guide for Early Years Foundation Stage Practitioners.* Ipswich: Suffolk County Council.

Kate Greenaway Nursery School and Children's Centre (2009) *Core Experiences for the Early Years Foundation Stage.* London: Kate Greenaway Nursery School and Children's Centre.

Liebschner, J. (1992) *A Child's Work: Freedom and Guidance in Froebel's Educational Theory and Practice.* Cambridge: Lutterworth.

Lilley, I. (1967) *Friedrich Froebel: A Selection from his Writings.* Cambridge: Cambridge University Press.

Lloyd Wright, F. (1943) *An Autobiography.* New York: Duell, Sloan & Pearce.

Louis, S. (2012) 'It's as easy as ABC (and D)': Froebel's principles in South African kindergartens. *Early Education,* 66 (Spring), 12–13.

Louis, S., Beswick, C., Magraw, L. and Hayes, L. (2008) *Again! Again! Understanding Schemas in Young Children.* London: A. & C. Black.

McCormick, C. (2012) Froebelian methods in a modern world: A case of cooking. In Bruce, T., *Early Childhood Practice: Froebel Today.* London: Sage.

Marenholtz-Bülow, B. von (1891) *Reminiscences of Friedrich Froebel* (translated by M. Mann). Boston: Lee & Shepard.

Middendorff, W. (1848) Die Kindergarten. In Owen, G. (1906) A study of the original kindergartens. *Elementary School Teacher,* 7(5), 206–207.

Milchem, K. (2011) Breaking through concrete: The emergence of Forest Schools in London. In Knight, S. (ed.) *Forest Schools for All.* London: Sage.

Ouvry, M. (2004) *Sounds Like Playing: Music and the Early Years Curriculum.* London: British Association of Early Childhood Education.

Ouvry, M. (2012) Froebel's Mother Songs today. In Bruce, T. (ed.) *Early Childhood Practice: Froebel Today.* London: Sage.

Parker, L. (2006) Exploring clay: A guide for early years practitioners. Unpublished MA Early Childhood Studies research project, Roehampton University, London.

Selleck, D. (2009) The Key Persons Approach in Reception Class. *Early Education*, 57(Spring), 3–5.

Spry, D., Latchford, P. and Hollis, A. (2010) *Nursery World*. 9 September, 18–19.

Stephenson, A. (2003) Physical risk taking: Dangerous or endangered? *Early Years*, 23(1), 35–43.

Tovey, H. (2007) *Playing Outdoors, Spaces and Places, Risk and Challenge.* Maidenhead: Open University Press.

Tovey, H. (2012) Adventurous and challenging play outdoors. In Bruce, T. (ed.) *Early Childhood Practice: Froebel Today.* London: Sage.

Trevarthen, C. (1995) The child's need to learn a culture. *Children and Society*, 9, 5–19.

Trudell, P. (2010) A place for play. In Moyles, J. *Thinking about Play: Developing a Reflective Approach.* Maidenhead: Open University Press.

Vygotsky, L. (1978) *Mind in Society.* Cambridge, MA: Harvard University Press.

Wells, G. (1986) *The Meaning Makers: Children Learning Language and Using Language to Learn.* Sevenoaks: Hodder & Stoughton.

Weston, P. (2000) *Friedrich Froebel: His Life, Times and Significance* (2nd edition). London: Roehampton Institute.

Whinnett, J. (2012) *Gifts and Occupations.* Froebel's gifts (wooden blockplay) and occupations (construction and workshop experiences) today. In Bruce, T. (ed.) *Early Childhood Practice: Froebel Today.* London: Sage.

Whitehead, M. (1995) Nonsense rhyme and word play in young children. In R. Beard (ed.) *Rhyme, Reading and Writing.* London: Hodder & Stoughton.

Whitehead, M. (2007) *Developing Language and Literacy with Young Children 0–8.* London: Paul Chapman.

Index

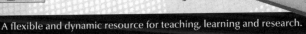